BACK to Pain-Free Health
Secrets of Natural Healing
for Back Pain

BACK to Pain-Free Health
Secrets of Natural Healing
for Back Pain

Dr. Mao Shing Ni, Ph.D, D.O.M., L.Ac.

and
Albert Vaca, L.Ac.

TAO OF
WELLNESS
PRESS

Published by
Tao of Wellness Press
An Imprint of SevenStar Communications
1412 14th Street,
Santa Monica, CA 90404
www. taoofwellness.com

ISBN 978-1-887575-24-9

Editing, page layout and design by Jordan Pomazon
Cover design by Justina Krakowski

A note to readers:
This book is intended to be informational and should not be considered a substitute for advice from a medical professional, whom the reader should consult before beginning any diet or exercise regiment, and before taking any dietary supplements or other medications. The author and publisher expressly disclaim responsibility for any adverse effects arising from the use or application of the information contained in this book.

We would like to thank Edsel Tan for his contributions to this book. Your invaluable input is greatly appreciated.

We also wish to thank Leah Jonas for coordinating this project from the inception to the very end. Her calm disposition, attention to details and dedication to our mission have been essential to bringing this and many other publications to fruition. This could not have happened without you.

This book is for those who've suffered the agony and indignity of back pain. We seek to empower you to heal and free you from your pain.

TABLE OF CONTENTS

Introduction

On her first visit, Beth arrived at our office with a cane and the agonizing look of someone who has been tormented by pain. Sure enough, she asked if she could stand during our initial consultation and evaluation—sitting was too uncomfortable. Five months ago, Beth had woken up with such horrible back pain that she couldn't get out of bed. The pain was so severe it made her nauseated. She cried for help, and her husband tried to help her out of bed but gave up quickly after seeing that Beth's pain only increased with every movement she made.

An urgent call was placed to Beth's physician, who referred her to an orthopedic specialist. The specialist prescribed several medications, including a muscle relaxant, an anti-inflammatory and narcotic. Beth felt a little better and was able to move. However, she couldn't sit or stand for more than 10 minutes without hot, scorching pain shooting from her right buttock down to her right calf. After one week with little relief from the drugs, the orthopedist ordered an x-ray and MRI which showed that Beth suffered from a herniated disc between her fourth and fifth lumbar vertebrae, with nerve compression on the right side. The scans also showed arthritic changes in the lumbar spine and bone spurs.

Beth underwent physical therapy for six weeks, but the pain persisted. So her orthopedist advised they proceed with an epidural block injection. After her first injection, Beth's pain was 90% better and she felt elated. However, after one week her pain returned with the same vengeance as before. Beth was devastated. Undeterred, she took another two epidural shots but did not experience the same relief. Since she failed to respond to the nerve block, her orthopedist recommended that she consider surgery to remove the portion of the disc that was pressing on the nerve and to widen the opening where the nerve emerged from the spine. Beth asked if there were any alternatives to surgery, and her physician suggested that acupuncture might be worth a shot and referred her to us at Tao of Wellness.

After a comprehensive exam and evaluation, our team formulated a treatment objective for Beth which included reducing inflammation and swelling of the disc, decompressing the nerve, increasing circulation in the lumbar spine area, relaxing muscles and reducing pain. The Chinese medicine treatment modality consisted of acupuncture with electrostimulation, tuina bodywork, cupping, gua sha, qi gong specifically designed for back pain, an anti-inflammatory diet and nutritional and herbal supplements such as papain and bromelain (enzymes that block inflammation) and myrrh and frankincense (herbs that increase circulation and block pain). At the end of the first month of treatments, Beth reported a pain reduction of about 30%. At the end of three months, her pain went from about an 8 out of 10 to a 2 out of 10. Her range of motion improved, as well as her ability to sit and stand for longer periods of time without aggravating her symptoms. Not only was she practicing qi gong for back pain, but she was also walking 25 minutes daily.

Six months after Beth started her acupuncture and Chinese medicine program at Tao of Wellness, she reported she was free of pain. A follow up a year later showed that she was still free of pain and had resumed her normal and active lifestyle. Beth's case was not an exception—she is one of thousands of patients who have come to Tao of Wellness over the last 30 years for their back pain conditions.

An estimated 80% of American men and women of various age groups suffer from periodic back pain, making it one of the most common reasons to visit primary care physicians in the United States and leading to an annual cost of nearly $20 billion in medical treatments and disability claims. More importantly, however, back pain is a hindrance to the overall quality of life. This is apparent when we consider that the average time to recover from back pain episodes is six to eight weeks and the pain is more likely to recur throughout our lives if we do not take appropriate action.

Why is back pain so common? The answer may lie in the fact that humans are bipedal, meaning we have an upright posture and walk with our legs.

The upright posture is maintained by muscle contractions and ligaments. The advantages of this far outweigh the disadvantages. An upright posture allows us to use our hands to carry objects and use tools. It also allows us to use a surprisingly small amount of energy. This efficiency enables the body to remain standing for many hours and to endure longer periods of walking and running.

Our well-developed brains and freed hands that resulted from our upright position have also allowed us to progress in science and technology. Being bipedal has allowed us to develop bicycles, boats, automobiles and airplanes, giving us the ability to travel faster and farther than any known species in the world.

The upright position does have a price, however. One disadvantage is slower speed compared to other species. The other disadvantage is the additional strain placed on joints not completely evolved to walk upright. Think of your entire trunk and head being supported by a stick made up of many small pieces joined together by rubber bands! The joints of the back are especially compromised. Over time, the effects of weight strain on these joints take its toll.

Technology has also sped up our rate of physical degeneration. We are less reliant on our bodies than ever, and more sedentary and physically weaker as a result. The average human today is vastly more frail than the average human of 100 years ago. The good news is that we can make a change. The first step is resolving any current back pain, and the second step is preventing its recurrence by returning to the strong, physically active beings we are meant to be.

In this book, we offer you a simple-to-follow program for eliminating back pain, based on over 40 years of cumulative clinical experience caring for back pain patients. After reading, you will understand not only how the back functions and how it is put together structurally, but also the importance of stretching and strengthening exercises called qi gong, as well as healthy postures for staying pain-free. We discuss integrative therapies for back problems, including mind-body connections, nutritional and herbal therapies and conventional allopathic and Eastern medical approaches to resolving pain due to various causes.

With stratospheric costs associated with caring for and living with back problems, we can't afford to continue in a business-as-usual fashion in dealing with it. Optimum back pain relief requires an integrative, holistic approach that addresses not only the symptomatic pain but also its root cause. By integrating proven and cost-effective therapeutic approaches, we are confident that sufferers, employers and society alike will be the beneficiaries of BACK to Pain-Free Health.

Chapter One

BACK to Basics:
Structure and Function

It's always helpful to understand the structure and function of something before you attempt to fix it. Your back is no exception. It is at once a simple and complex system of bones, muscles, nerves and vessels. The invisible but essential part of the tree anatomy is the xylem tubes inside that transport water and nutrients from the root to the rest of the tree trunk, branch, leaves and flower. The bones in your back support and frame your body, arms and legs. The muscles, tendons and ligaments are the rubber bands that keep your bones together and allow you to stand and walk upright. The nerves connect the brain to the rest of your body, including all your organs, and give you the ability to move, sense and perform the intricate dance of life. The vessels that transport nutrients and wastes lubricate, protect and heal injuries are what keeps your structure alive and functioning optimal. All the pieces fit together like a puzzle and work elegantly and practically. However, when there is breakdown in any part of this system due to trauma, weakness, infection or another reason, pain is the first warning.

In this chapter you will learn about the most common causes of back pain. The information is intended to help you develop a better understanding of your own pain. Once you have a better insight into your specific condition, I suggest you follow the program outlined in the rest of the book as well as seek consultation with a licensed acupuncturist or qualified integrative health care professional for precise diagnostics and treatment.

The Backstory of your Back

Your backside consists of five primary regions: neck/cervical, trunk/thoracic, lower back/lumbar, sacrum, and tailbone/coccyx. This system includes bones, cartilage, intervertebral discs, ligaments, tendons, muscles, and nerves all relating to the spinal cord, which is the primary nerve bundle that connects to the brain. The spinal cord and brain make up our central nervous system—the hub of our physical, mental and physiological being. The central nervous system serves as the foundation to our existence. When the back is impaired, every aspect of our lives is affected including our physical, mental and emotional well-being.

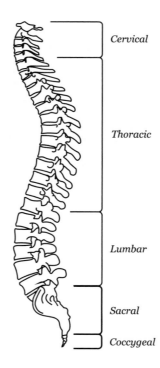

Cervical

Thoracic

Lumbar

Sacral

Coccygeal

Meatball on a Stick

If an alien visited our planet and took a look at you, it might appear that that your head is like a meatball being propped up by a bamboo stick. In reality the stick, your spine, is comprised of 33 bones and is the structural foundation of the human body. The vertebral column of the human back protects the spinal cord, the primary nerve bundle that joins the brain in what is referred to as the central nervous system.

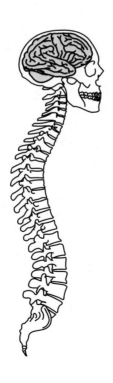

The Signals of Life - Qi

The brain controls all essential physiological functions, physical movement and sensory perception through the spinal cord. The spinal cord connects the brain to all nerve endings throughout the human body. The human organism is brought to life by electromagnetic signals initiated in the brain and distributed through the central nervous system.

A healthy back allows those vital neural signals that in Chinese medicine, we call them qi or vital energy to travel through the central nervous system and enable our physiological functions, physical movement, and sensory interaction with the universe. Qi energy is the signal of life for without it life as we know it ceases to exist. Taking all this into consideration, it is clear that a healthy back is important for quality and longevity of life.

One Reason for Five-Inch Stilettos

Ever wondered what humans would look like without a back or spine? The spine makes up two-fifths of the total height of most people. The bones of the back are the seven cervical vertebrae (neck), twelve thoracic vertebrae (trunk), five lumbar vertebrae (lower back), five fused sacral vertebrae (sacrum) and the four coccygeal vertebrae (tailbone). In between each vertebrae are intervertebral discs that act as soft shock absorbers. If the spaces between your vertebrae decrease, you will become shorter. This is unfortunately very common in old age if you don't have a strong and healthy back. Add in osteoporosis and it is not uncommon to see people in their eighties lose up to five inches in height. That explains the five-inch stiletto!

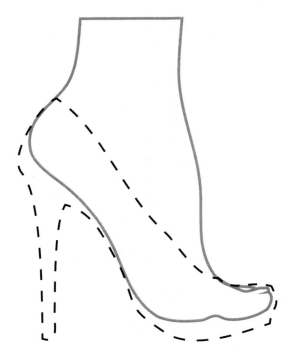

Your Curves Are Beautiful

The back has four primary curves: two forward curves in the neck and lower back and two backward curves in the thoracic back and sacrum. If the curves are gradual and distribute weight evenly, they actually help to increase the strength of the back, provide balance while standing or sitting upright, absorb pressure from our day to day activities, and help protect the spine from traumatic injury.

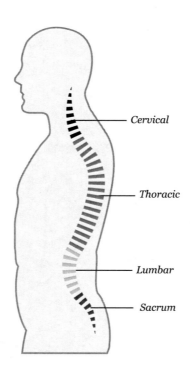

Cervical

Thoracic

Lumbar

Sacrum

The Not-So-Beautiful Curves

Abnormal curvatures occur when the back is curved laterally (to the right or left) or if the forward and backward curvatures are excessive, which leads to painful straining of the muscles and tendons. When the back is curved like a "S" from side to side it is called scoliosis. When the neck or lower back are curved too far forward these phenomenons are called kyphosis or lordosis respectively. If left untreated or uncorrected these abnormal curvatures of the spine can lead to lifelong back pain.

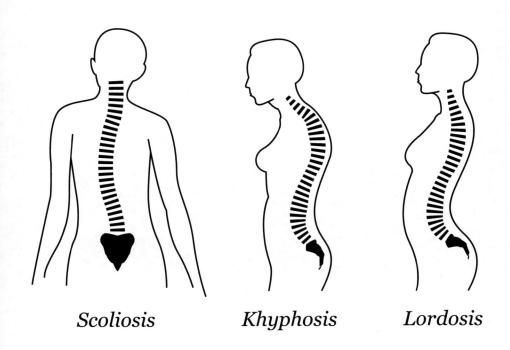

Scoliosis   *Khyphosis*   *Lordosis*

The Lego Pieces of Your Back

Your vertebrae are stacked on top of one another like Lego pieces to support the weight of the head and trunk. They have different sizes and shapes depending on where they are located. Each vertebrae consists of two parts: body and arch.

Your Vertebrae and Oreo Cookies

The vertebral body is a drum-shaped section located at the front of the spine. The top and bottom surfaces of the vertebral body are called end plates. Between the end plates are where the intervertebral discs—or the "shock absorbers"—are located. Imagine the vertebral body as an Oreo cookie—the disc is the cream in between.

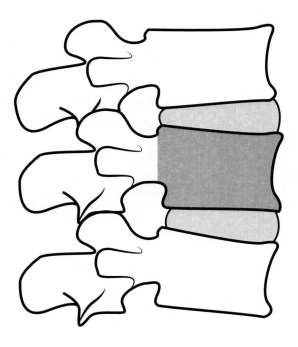

The Arch Angels and Facets of Our Back

The vertebral arch is located at the back of the spine. The vertebral arch is shaped like a triangle and resembles archangels with pointed arches.

The vertebral arch features structures called facets which literally means "little faces" (two on the top surface and two on the bottom surface). The facets of adjacent vertebrae join together to form the joints that support the back and prevent slippage of one vertebra over another.

Facet joints help stabilize the spine and limit excessive motion that would put the spinal cord in danger. The facet joints are lined with cartilage and are surrounded by a lubricated capsule that enables the spine to bend and twist. Stress on these facets can generate pain.

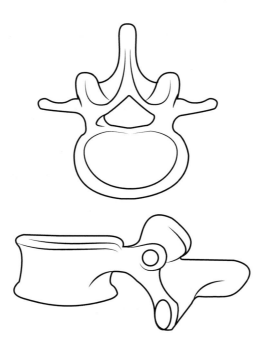

Stenosis Means Narrowing of the Spinal Opening

The space between the vertebral body and arch forms the spinal canal and vertebral foramen—or the opening through which the spinal cord and nerve roots pass respectively. Narrowing of the spinal opening is called stenosis, which can cause a great deal of pain. This is just one reason why it's imperative that you maintain the health of your vertebrae.

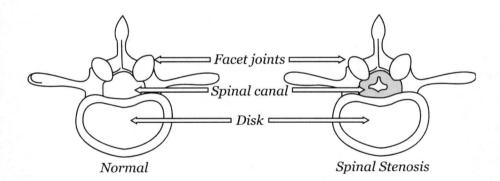

Facet joints

Spinal canal

Disk

Normal   *Spinal Stenosis*

The Pelvic Girdle Is Like a Planter

The foundation of the spine is the pelvic girdle. Using the bamboo analogy, the pelvic girdle is the container in which the trunk is planted, allowing upright support as well as bending without toppling over. This foundation is a movable yet stable structure through which the body's weight is distributed. The pelvic girdle is the connecting point of the top and bottom halves of the body. It consists of the sacrum and the hip that connects to the thighs. The girdle is comprised of five joints: the two joints on each side that connect the sacrum to the pelvis, the two joints that connect the hip bones to the thigh bones, and the single joint (symphysis pubis) that connects the two halves of the pelvis in the front.

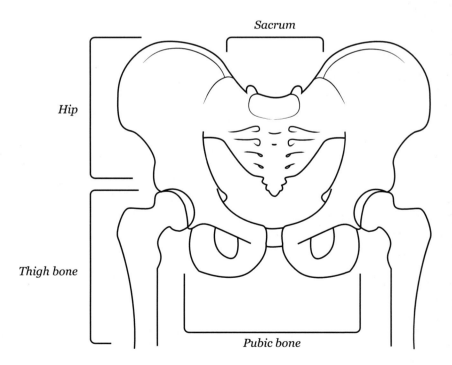

Sacrum

Hip

Thigh bone

Pubic bone

Don't Become the Leaning Tower of Pisa

As you stand and sit, the ligaments that connect the sacrum to the pelvic girdle at the sacroiliac joints have to stay somewhat elastic. But when this joint bears weight, the ligaments tighten making the pelvic girdle very stable. The angle of the pelvic tilt affects the curvature of the spine. This angle is a critical determining factor of your posture. If the angle of the pelvic tilt is correct, then the curves of the spine will be balanced and stable. If the angle of your pelvic tilt is incorrect, poor posture and consequent back injury is usually the result. A severe tilt may even make you look like the leaning tower of Pisa.

Discs Are the Shock Absorbers

The intervertebral discs are located on the upper and lower surfaces of the vertebral bodies, from the second cervical vertebrae all the way down to the sacrum. They are the shock absorbers of the back, absorbing the force of day-to-day activities and enabling the spine to move freely. Without the discs, the force transferred throughout the body could possibly fracture the vertebrae and vibrate the brain to the point of injury.

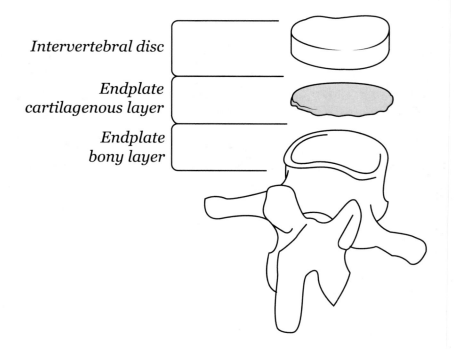

Intervertebral disc

Endplate cartilagenous layer

Endplate bony layer

We Would Be a Lot Shorter Without Our Discs

Each disc has a fibrous outer layer and a soft, gelatinous core that
absorbs fluid. This core usually enlarges when pressure on the
disc is lessened. Consequently, we are often taller upon waking
than we are after a long day of work. On the other hand, the discs
naturally shrink through time. Habitually neglecting to drink
enough water can speed up the degeneration of these discs. As
a result, instead of a soft and gelatinous core, you might have
a harder core that presses on the outer fibrous layer with more
force, leading to tears that leave you more vulnerable to bulging
or herniated discs—one of the primary causes of back injury and
pain.

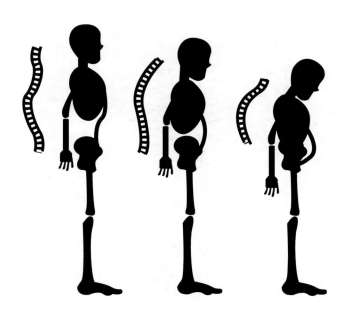

The Spinal Cord—
A Two-Way Street Between the Brain and the Body

The spinal cord is a bundle of nerve tissue that travels from the base of the brain, through the spinal canal, ending at the first and second lumbar vertebrae of the lower back. The spinal cord is the primary pathway through which the brain and the rest of the body communicate with each other. Through 31 pairs of nerve roots branching off the spinal cord, the brain is able to transmit commands to the various organs and muscles. Yet, the nervous system is a two-way street, since the various tissues of the body are also able to send signals to the brain and elicit an appropriate response.

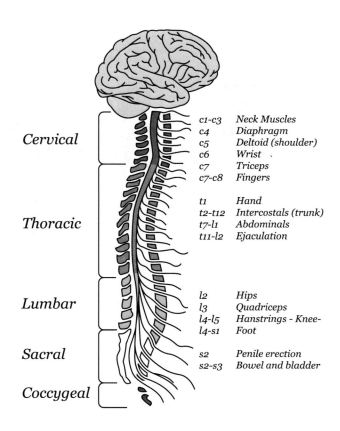

c1-c3	*Neck Muscles*
c4	*Diaphragm*
c5	*Deltoid (shoulder)*
c6	*Wrist*
c7	*Triceps*
c7-c8	*Fingers*
t1	*Hand*
t2-t12	*Intercostals (trunk)*
t7-l1	*Abdominals*
t11-l2	*Ejaculation*
l2	*Hips*
l3	*Quadriceps*
l4-l5	*Hanstrings - Knee-*
l4-s1	*Foot*
s2	*Penile erection*
s2-s3	*Bowel and bladder*

Cervical

Thoracic

Lumbar

Sacral

Coccygeal

The Ups and Downs of Your Nerve Signals

There are two types of nerve signals. Those that travel from your body to the brain are called ascending. Pain, for example, is an ascending signal that makes us aware of tissue irritation or injury. Sensory signals are also ascending, providing our minds with essential information through sight, smell, sound, taste, and touch.

Descending signals travel from the brain to a system within the body. There are two types of descending signals: motor and autonomic. Motor signals travel from the brain through the motor nerves of the spinal cord to the appropriate musculoskeletal system to enable movement. Autonomic signals travel from the brain through the autonomic nerves of the spinal cord to regulate involuntary physiological functions, such as intestinal movement and heartbeat. This is the autopilot that enables us to stay alive without thinking about it. Irritation or damage to spinal cord nerves can manifest as pain anywhere in the body, including the back.

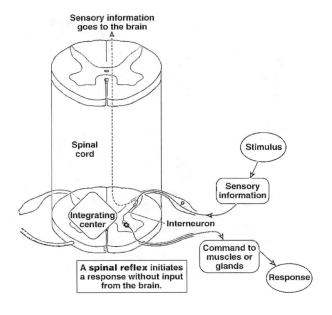

The Nerve Root of Back Pain and Dysfunction

Nerve bundles consist of sensory nerves, motor nerves, autonomic nerves, or a mixture of the three. Irritation or damage of the nerves of the spinal cord can manifest as pain anywhere in the body. Such an injury can also lead to excessive contraction of a particular body tissue. If a spinal nerve injury leads to an excessive contraction or spasm, sensory nerves become over-stimulated, circulation of blood is obstructed, and nourishment to the tissue is depleted. Without nourishment, the tissue becomes weak and more vulnerable to injury. The injury then releases inflammatory chemicals that irritate pain receptors that consequently send pain signals to the brain. Additionally, nerve damage can also lead to an insufficient function of a particular muscle tissue and consequently, weakness, atrophy, or paralysis may result. This weakness also leaves one more vulnerable to injury and pain.

Bulging Disc Pressing on Nerve

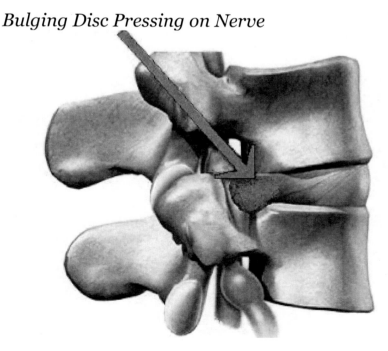

The Glue That Holds the Skeleton Together

Both ligaments and tendons are made up of collagen. Ligaments and tendons connect to the front and backside of the vertebrae and keep the spine as one continuous unit. Tendons connect muscle to bone and ligaments connect bone to bone. They are durable, fibrous bands of collagen that support the joints and keep them in alignment to prevent injury. Ligaments and tendons are the glue that holds the skeleton together as a whole. When exaggerated movements on a joint are severe, ligaments can tear and become inflamed and this injury can result in pain.

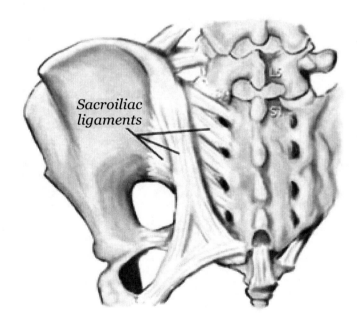

Sacroiliac ligaments

Spasms Are the Bane of Muscle's Existence

Muscular contraction causes the tendons to pull on your bones, for either movement or stabilization. An abnormal muscle contraction is called a spasm. Tendons actually have special sensory nerves that restrict muscle when the pull on the tendon is too strong. As the muscle becomes tighter from either stress tension or injury, they pull on the tendon with greater force, increasing the risk of fraying and tearing and consequently inflammation of the tendon or tendinitis. Inflammation leads to the release of chemicals that activate local pain receptors. Tendinitis thus leads to joint pain, including pain in the joints of the back.

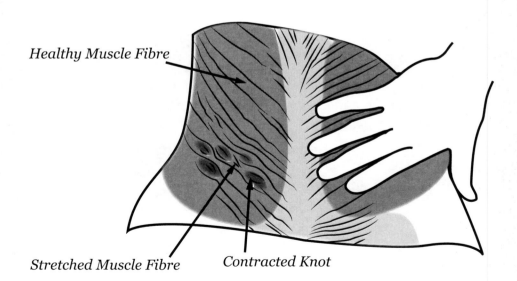

Healthy Muscle Fibre

Stretched Muscle Fibre   *Contracted Knot*

The Magnitude of Spinal Support Muscles

Your back muscles are part of the spinal support muscles that attach to the spine and are responsible for moving and stabilizing the back as well as your abdominal core. Spinal support muscles also include muscles of the abdominal region, buttocks, hips, and legs. Engaging spinal support muscles allow us to carry out an infinite variety of movement as well as keeping the back aligned.

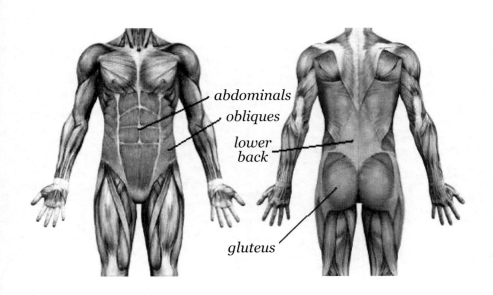

abdominals

obliques

lower back

gluteus

Strong Abs Keep Your Back Well

The abdominal muscle group, in particular, is a type of spinal support muscle that is extremely important for the prevention and rehabilitation of back injury. We have four sets of abdominal muscles that surround the lower torso and serve as the connection between the pelvis and the ribs. This muscular system is essential for stabilizing the spine, especially during the most basic bending and twisting movements.

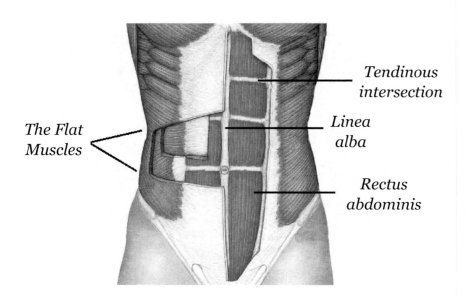

Tendinous intersection

The Flat Muscles

Linea alba

Rectus abdominis

The Connectors Between Your Pelvis and Legs

The muscles of the hips, buttocks and legs, including the psoas, hip flexors, gluts, piriformis, quadriceps and hamstrings, support the back by controlling the degree of pelvic tilt, consequently affecting your posture. This group of muscles connect your legs to your pelvis, and spasms or looseness can throw your posture off. A balanced distribution of force leads to a strong healthy back, whereas the opposite causes pain and dysfunction.

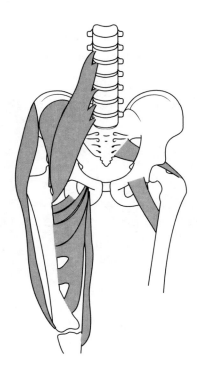

The Link Between the Back and the Core

The back is fundamental to the core of the human body. The major muscle groups of the core are the diaphragm, the pelvic floor, the abdominal muscles, and the muscles of the mid and lower back. The core is instrumental to maintaining both static core and dynamic core functions. Static core function is the alignment of the body skeleton to the force of gravity, allowing for more efficient use of energy. In other words, maintaining proper posture.

Dynamic core function is the basis of all movement. The back stabilizes the body in motion, integrating postural reactions to changes in speed, motion, and power. Bending and straightening your body requires the normal functioning of both back and core muscles. If the core is weak, then the back compensates, causing it to become tight and strained. This is one of the most common causes of back pain. (In Chapter 5, you will learn exercise and qi gong practices that strengthen your core.)

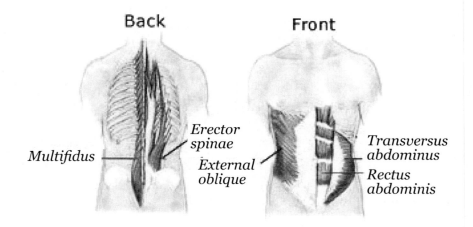

The Top of the Lacrosse Stick—Your Neck

The neck is a vital area of the body. It is a corridor for all our vital substances: air, food, blood, and nerves that transport signals throughout the body. The neck is also the platform for the head and brain. Because of the neck's importance, injury impacts the rest of your back and body. Certain neck pain can be linked to injury of the lower sections of the spine, since the whole spine is an integrated unit that is literally linked together. This means that pain and injury of the upper, middle, and lower back can spread to the neck. Furthermore, pain and injury can also start at the neck and spread down to the upper, middle and lower back. On the other hand, when the neck is healthy, the whole body system is optimized.

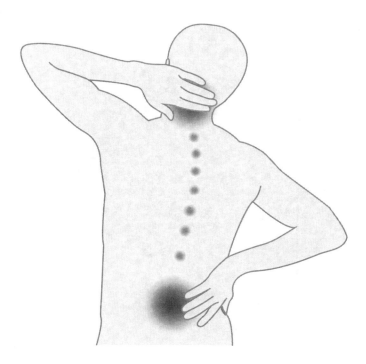

Why You May Be a Pain in Your Neck

The neck must do a great deal of work. The muscles in the back of the neck bring the head backward. The muscles in the sides of the neck bend the neck laterally. These muscles also rotate the head and neck. The muscles in the front of the neck bring the head forward. The muscles between the shoulder blades support the weight of the head. An average head weighs 10–15 pounds. Poor posture with improper placement of your head can add additional weight strain to your neck. For example bending your head at 45 degrees forward for extended period of time will more than triple the weight burden of 49 pounds to your neck. The constant weight of the head bearing down on the neck and the countless head movements we do on a given day may cause strains and inflammation that can constrict blood circulation and slow down healing, which in turn stresses and injures ligaments that aggravate muscle strains. This vicious circle is why people suffer from chronic neck pain that sometimes persists for decades.

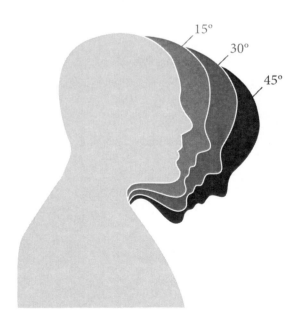

Chapter Two

Common Conditions
of the Neck and Back

Pain, especially when it occurs in the back, causes people to either stop in their tracks, get help or turn to something that allows them avoid it. It is a powerful motivator. Pain informs us that an injury has occurred. The pain receptors of the back are stimulated by chemical changes, inflammatory responses and structural factors that result from back injury. Through the pain receptors, pain signals are sent to the brain. Back pain can be acute or chronic and vary in degree of frequency and severity. Emotional pain and physical pain can aggravate one another.

Four out of five people will experience back pain at least once in their lives. The World Health Organization states that some form of back pain affects 80% of people some time during their lives. Back pain is one of the most common reasons that people go to the doctor or lose work.

Why Do You Have Pain?

The function of back pain is to let us know that the back is injured. Symptoms of pain are the last thing to manifest. Your body has already been experiencing a malfunction and it has gotten to the point where it is screaming for help. In fact, pain protects you from doing something harmful to further injure yourself. Once you know that you have an injury, you are more likely to get help and eventually heal from it.

When Should You Seek Help?

- You've been managing the pain yourself for more than three days with no improvement.

- The back pain radiates down the arms and legs or you feel numbness and tingling in the arms and legs.

- You've had a physically traumatic incident preceding the back pain.

- You're over the age of fifty and this is your first experience with back pain at this level of severity and frequency.

- You experience problems with the bowel or urinary bladder.

- You feel abdominal pain.

- You feel feverish.

- You have a history of other chronic illnesses that could be related to the back pain you're feeling.

Go for a Thorough Investigation

When a healthcare provider meets the back pain sufferer for the first time, a series of topics should be addressed. For one, the provider should know how long the back pain has been occurring. History of any traumatic injury must be taken into consideration. The quality of the pain should be discussed. For instance, a provider may ask if the pain is an acute, sharp, localized, burning, irritating pain or a chronic, sore, vague, nagging ache. Knowing whether or not the back pain radiates down an arm or leg is also significant.

Besides physical examination your provider may order tests, including but not limited to x-ray, MRI (magnetic resonance imaging) and CT scan (computed tomography). When symptoms of extremities are involved tests such as Needle EMG (electromyography) or NCS (nerve conduction study) may also be ordered to assess the health of the muscle and nerves.

What Makes Your Pain Worse

Aggravating factors should be identified as well as relieving factors. History of treatment is an important element to understanding the current pain as well as the level of relief and the therapeutic effect of each of the previous and current treatments. The patient's complete medical history may also be reviewed and analyzed thoroughly. The back pain sufferer's diet and lifestyle should also be discussed and taken into consideration, as well as one's emotional state.

Additional factors that worsen your pain such as prolonged sitting, standing, weight bearing, lying down, bending forward, backward and to the sides, reaching up, hot, cold, constipation, premenstrual for women, and urinary difficulty can all offer clues to your healthcare provider for more accurate diagnosis.

A Good Doctor Observes

This part of the evaluation begins with the provider making either a mental or written note of posture, body type, muscle tone, soft tissues, gait, and the overall comfort level of the patient. Such key observations are essential to an accurate diagnosis and appropriate treatment for resolving back pain.

Chinese medicine practitioners take a step further with observation by inspecting the patient's tongue which reflects the condition of your entire body. This is called tongue mapping and can reveal hidden causes of your illness.

Physical Examination Is Key

Physical tests help the provider to achieve a more specific understanding of the patient's back pain. A provider may apply a physical examination to observe the joint integrity and mobilization of the back. The provider may also apply physical examination to observe active movements upon pressure on the affected area. A more precise observation of muscles may be done through tests measuring strength, control, length and isometric contraction. Physical tests may also be done to observe neurological integrity.

When a patient comes to the Tao of Wellness, our team of acupuncture physicians often begin by examining or palpating the back. We feel for misalignment of joints or tender articulations which may elicit pain sensations. We palpate the muscle of the affected area. Muscles of the injured area or related to the injured area may be hypertonic, meaning overly tense, stiff and spastic. Such a texture in muscle tissue is a drain to an individual's energy, and this prolonged state of contraction can eventually lead to a biochemical imbalance that can spread to surrounding areas.

When Your Muscles Are Too Tense

Hypertonic muscles can imply obstruction of blood vessels, which hinders blood circulation. Obstruction of blood can also slow the healing process, since blood is unable to nourish the injured area with nutrients and oxygen. Furthermore, hypertonic muscles that are constantly contracted can lead to inflammation that can consequently lead to irritation of nerves and pain receptors, and therefore increase pain to the level that affects quality of life.

Hypertonic muscles can also contribute to a progressively decreased range of motion of the back. The tendons and ligaments of the injured joint can lose elasticity, tighten up, and further degrade motion. And as joints remain fixed, stagnation persists and worsens. We also identify atrophy and/or the underdevelopment of muscle groups in the back that can potentially lead to weakness and back pain. Finally, we palpate the skin of the back to feel for heat or cold.

Pulse Diagnosis—a Subtle But Insightful Exam

Acupuncturists use palpation of the pulse to identify diagnostic information in deciding the root cause and manifestations of back pain. If the resting pulse is predominantly hyperactive, this indicates that the pathogenic mechanism is also hyperactive in nature. If the pulse is predominantly hypoactive, this indicates that the pathogenic mechanism stems from a root cause of deficiency or weakness. A pulse is hyperactive when it is surging, wiry and/or tight. A pulse is hypoactive when it is weak, deep and thin. An acupuncturist may also pay attention to the quality of the pulse, for this indicates certain physiological conditions of an organ system or of a combination of organ systems that may be contributing to the individual's back pain. Besides the pulse texture, we also palpate for the resting pulse rate, which provides information regarding your general cardiovascular health.

Through the Looking Glass—Imaging Tests

X-ray is electromagnetic radiation in the form of photon particles passed through the examined area of the body. A computer or special film is used to record the images that are created. Dense structures such as bone and special dyes appear white. Structures containing air appear black. Muscle, fat and fluid appear as shades of gray. With back pain patients, this form of imaging is typically used to examine bony structures.

MRI or magnetic resonance imaging uses a magnetic field, radio waves and a computer to produce images of body structures that do not appear in an x-ray. Doctors can examine the brain, spinal cord, intervertebral discs and even the heat of major blood vessels. MRI is also useful in examining the organs of the abdominal cavity, joints, soft tissue and bones.

CT/CAT scan, or computerized tomography, is imaging of cross-sections of anatomical structures, using an x-ray unit that rotates around the body and a powerful computer. This imaging shows the detailed inner structure of the examined body structure. This is especially useful in examining bone disorders such as bone tumors and fractures.

A bone scan uses a radioactive tracer that is injected into a vein, then travels through the blood stream and into the bones. A special camera that picks up gamma waves takes pictures with the tracer in the bone. Cold spots appear dark, because only small amounts of tracer are absorbed. Hot spots appear bright because increased amounts are absorbed in these areas. Cold spots can indicate areas of bone that lack blood supply. Hot spots can indicate areas of possible arthritis, tumor, fracture or infection. EMG (electromyography) is a test that measures the electrical activity of the nerves that control certain muscles. This is helpful in diagnosing nerve compression or nerve injury.

Don't Delay, Get Help Today

If you have suffered from back pain and continue to suffer, it is time to take action. Delayed action may worsen your condition and can sometimes be fatal if it's cancerous. Take time to research and understand the aggravating factors of your back pain. Make a decision to get well today and commit to the most appropriate treatment plan with the help of an integrative team of healthcare providers, which may include acupuncture and Chinese medicine doctors, osteopathic doctors, chiropractic doctors, orthopedists, physical therapists and psychotherapists. Execute the treatment plan with dedication and commitment and above all, keep a positive mental attitude. Persevere until you are pain-free or find a successful coping mechanism.

WHIPLASH

Whiplash Isn't Just From Car Accidents

Whiplash is a soft tissue injury of the neck that involves pain and spasm, typically spreading from the base of the skull through all regions of the neck, trapezius, shoulder and upper back. It is a result of a force of impact causing the torso to aggressively move forward and upward as the neck extends, compresses and recoils—all within 1/10 of second. Such an event traumatizes the muscles of the neck and sometimes even the ligaments, intervertebral discs and facet joints. The severity of the injury generally depends on the amount of force of impact. Whiplash is a neck injury that is common amongst those who have been in automobile accidents. Whiplash may also occur in such contact sports such as football, rugby and hockey.

The Delayed Response

The pain may not occur immediately. The surge of endorphins and adrenaline occurs to help the body manage the stress of being in an accident. Endorphins and adrenaline also suppress pain, yet their levels usually drop off within 24 hours. Consequently, the pain and inflammation become more and more noticeable. Whiplash, however, may not surface until days, weeks, months or even years later if left untreated. Immediate integrative care can prevent this injury from getting worse.

Healing With Acupuncture

Acupuncture has been found to be extremely effective in relieving whiplash. Typically, it is applied to tender points of the neck, trapezius, shoulder and upper back to reduce tension, improve blood circulation, initiate an anti-inflammatory reaction and relieve pain, therefore accelerating the healing of damaged tissue and allowing an easier, more complete recovery. Acupuncture is best applied as soon as possible to help prevent the injury from penetrating into the deeper tissue and structures.

Healing With Tuina Bodywork

Tuina bodywork is also used to assist and accelerate the healing process. Tuina (pronounced "twee-nah") is Chinese Medical massage that removes blockages along the meridians of the body and stimulates the healthy flow of chi (vital energy), lymph and blood. This energizes the patient's innate self-healing mechanism. Tuina encompasses a broad range of techniques ranging from light stroking to deep tissue work and often employs joint mobilization and stretching techniques. It is a unique type of therapeutic bodywork that is based on principles of Chinese medicine and fully integrated into your acupuncture treatment plan.

Healing With Cupping

Cupping has been a part of Chinese medical bodywork for thousands of years, and also has been practiced in Eastern Europe for centuries. It involves using ceramic, wooden or glass cups or jars that when lit with fire on the inside create a negative pressure or suction. When applied to the back or other parts of the body, these heated cups increase circulation and healing. Cupping is often used for muscle spasm in the back with immediate results. At the 2016 summer Olympics in Brazil, Michael Phelps and his teammates on the US Olympic Swim Team were seen spotted with cupping marks on their back—they were using cupping to quickly recover quickly from their competitions. Such was the healing power of this thousand-year old Chinese medical procedure!

Healing With Gua Sha

Another common technique within Chinese medicine is Gua Sha, which involves using a tool made from oxen or antelope horn that is shaped like a solid hair comb. The comb is used in a scraping and stroking motion against the skin to activate release of lactic acid (a waste irritant from the muscle fibers), increase micro-capillary circulation and stimulate immune response. Therefore, Gua Sha is used commonly and effectively to help heal back pain and other soft tissue injuries. It is also used in pediatric care to treat the common cold, sinus congestion, ear infections, bronchitis and asthma. An important note is that for Gua Sha to be most effective it must be administered by licensed acupuncturists as it should be practiced strictly according to Chinese medical principles.

Healing With Herbal Therapy

Herbal therapy is an integral part of Chinese medicine. It harnesses nature's healing powers to help you recover from musculoskeletal injuries. There are many herbs that possess anti-inflammatory, antispasmodic and analgesic properties that may be familiar to you. These include turmeric, a common spice found in curry, Cat's Claw, an herb for muscle spasm and white willow bark, commonly used for pain. Chinese herbal therapy combines up to 12-15 natural plants working synergistically in a formula to restore health and wellness. The majority of herbs have been used for thousands of years and are proven to be safe and effective. However, always work with a reputable licensed acupuncturist and doctor of Chinese medicine to have your formulas customized for your body type and condition.

Healing With Nutritional Therapy

As early as 4,000 years ago in recorded Chinese history, nutritional therapy was recognized as a first line of defense against illness as well as integral to the healing process. Similar to herbal treatment, you can speed up recovery with the right kinds of foods or worsen your condition with the wrong kinds of foods. For example, ginger, pineapple and papaya are naturally anti-inflammatory while tomato, potato and cow milk products increase inflammation. Papain, bromelain and Co-Q10 are supplements that reduce inflammation and help muscle repair and are safe to combine with drugs.

STINGER

A Stinger Is Not From Bees

A stinger is a bruise of a nerve root, located in the neck where the root exits the spinal cord. It is caused by traumatic force applied to the neck while it is extended and flexed sideways. This injury is specific to contact sports that involve tackling, full body blocking and takedowns such as American football and grappling sports like wrestling, judo and martial arts. It may also occur while skiing or snowboarding if the athlete were to accidentally collide with a tree or another person.

Symptoms include a burning sensation that begins in the neck and radiates down the arm on the affected side. Stingers are not usually felt on both sides of the body. Numbness, tingling and weakness that extend down the neck, shoulders and arm are associated with stingers. The symptoms usually come and go and are not constant. Stingers should not affect the range of motion of the neck.

Acupuncture immediately following injury can usually provide instant relief. You can also prevent stingers from recurring by lengthening and strengthening the neck and shoulder muscles on a regular basis. The exercises described in Chapter 5 incorporate certain movements to help achieve healing.

MUSCLE SPRAINS AND STRAINS

Sprain and Strains That May Break Your Back

Muscles, tendons and ligaments are susceptible to being stressed beyond their healthy ranges of pliability. Such stress is especially likely during high levels of physical activity. A sprain is a tear of a ligament and a strain is a tear of a muscle or a tendon. These tears can vary in degrees of severity. The severity of the tear influences the length of the recovery time.

The primary symptom of a sprain or strain of the back is a spasm. A spasm is an uncontrollable, abnormal contraction of muscle. When the excessive contraction occurs near the spinal cord or nerve roots, pain is the result. Sometimes, this pain is extreme and debilitating and is worse with any movement. Torn muscles create inflammation that results in additional pressure and irritation of the nerves. The inflammation can also stretch the initial tear, consequently aggravating the pain.

R.I.C.E. vs. R.A.S.H.

Traditionally it has been recommended that you practice rest, ice, compression and elevation (R.I.C.E.) for the first 72 hours upon the onset of sprain, strain or spasm. However, Chinese medicine has differed on this advice and has long offered rest, activate with tuina bodywork, stabilize and heat (R.A.S.H.) to improve blood circulation to the affected area. In clinical practice we have found that both work well depending on the condition. For instance, if the sprain and strain caused severe swelling, ice and compression can quickly control the swelling so that the bodywork can then activate blood flow. Likewise, a sprain that results in spasm and is absent of swelling should be applied with heat to relax the muscles and speed up the recovery.

NSAIDs Are OK Short Term But Only With Food

The moderate use of over-the-counter non-steroidal anti-inflammatory drugs (NSAIDs) can also be helpful in bringing down acute inflammation, spasm and pain during the first 72 hours of injury, if you have no allergies or gastrointestinal sensitivities to such medication. The four NSAIDS most often taken for neck and back pain include aspirin, ibuprofen, naproxen and celeboxib. However, it is recommended that the use of NSAIDs be short term and always taken with a full stomach to protect against drug-induced gastritis and ulcer.

Healing With Natural Medicine

Acupuncture, tuina bodywork, an anti-inflammatory diet and herbal therapy are the preferred and first line of treatment for back sprain, strain and spasm because they are natural and free of side effects. As previously discussed, these treatments are effective in relieving tension, promoting blood circulation and reducing pain. With the above healing modalities, the pain should be reduced with five to eight consecutive treatments. If not, an orthopedic physician or neurologist may be consulted to rule out more serious injury. If no resolution is achieved in one month, diagnostic imaging may be ordered to investigate the problem further.

Go Further With Non-Invasive, Complementary Therapies

If more serious injury is ruled out and yet pain and muscle spasm persist, a more potent anti-inflammatory medication, muscle relaxant, and non-invasive therapies such as physical therapy, osteopathic manipulation and chiropractic treatment may be integrated with natural treatments. Rehabilitative exercise and qi gong can also be incorporated under the supervision of a physical therapist and certified instructor, respectively.

When you have achieved a full range of motion and are free of pain after basic activities, a gradual return to sports and more rigorous exercise is appropriate. If pain returns, you should reduce sports and rigorous activity. Four to six weeks is a standard time span to recover fully from back sprain, strain and spasm.

Subluxation of Vertebrae and Dislocation of Joints

Spasm in the back can persist and progress to the point that the alignment of the vertebrae (back bones) is altered. The articular surfaces of the back bones that normally fit together perfectly to form a joint can be pulled slightly out of alignment by tense, spastic muscles. As a result, the rehabilitation of the spasm is hindered, and as muscle remains spastic and shortened, the back becomes vulnerable to osteoarthritis, disc injury, nerve irritation and worsening pain.

Structure Follows Function

Ever wonder how acupuncture can be effective for structural issues like subluxation and dislocation? This is an example of form follows function. Acupuncture helps to relieve tension and spasm in the muscle and restores pliability and tone, therefore allowing the vertebrae and joints to be restored to their proper placement. For structural problems, acupuncture works well in collaboration with manual therapies such as tuina bodywork, chiropractic, and osteopathy that are focused in restoring the affected joint to its normal range of motion and optimum alignment. Such manual therapies are more effective if muscle tension is first reduced by acupuncture.

OSTEOARTHRITIS

Osteoarthritis Is Wear and Tear of Cartilage in the Joint

Osteoarthritis is the degeneration of joints caused by varying degrees of wear and tear of cartilage. Cartilage provides a smooth, protective lining on joint surfaces, but is consistently worn away through various motions and activities. Normally, worn-out cartilage is replaced by fresh cartilage. Yet, cartilage-producing cells within the joints can be worn down to the point that these cells form irregular surfaces within the joint. This results to more friction within the joint surfaces, which leads to more osteoarthritis. This is a chronic process that is more common in people over 60, although those who have experienced physical trauma in any part of the back are predisposed. The neck is more prone to osteoarthritis than the rest of the back because it has more mobility and less structural support and therefore more wear and tear.

The Story of Nerve Compression, Spurs and Degeneration

Osteoarthritis may progress to degenerative intervertebral discs and to irregular surfaces in the bone. These irregular surfaces are called bone spurs or osteophytes. In more serious cases, these irregular bone surfaces can narrow the spinal canal. This is called spinal stenosis. They can also narrow the space between the vertebrae where nerve roots travel, called the foramina. When this occurs, it is called radiculopathy. Compressed nerve roots can lead to severe, stabbing pain that radiates down an arm or leg. Joint degeneration can further progress to the point where one vertebra fuses with another.

Stiffness in the Morning and Pain in the Evening

Symptoms of osteoarthritis include pain and limited range of motion in the affected joint. The joint pain is usually a constant ache and is typically worse in the morning and in the evening. The joint pain can also irritate the surrounding muscles and ligaments, causing these soft tissues to tighten up and inflame. Inflammation leads to the release of chemicals into the surrounding area that lead to further tissue irritation and inflammation. Consequently, inflammation creates a physical pressure on blood vessels and decreases circulation. As blood flow decreases, the supply of nutrients and oxygen is affected, leading to an energy crisis within the affected joint and the surrounding area. Without optimum blood flow, healing is negatively impacted and degeneration is progressively worsened.

Studies show that acupuncture is effective in reducing inflammation, increase circulation and decrease pain and is recommended by National Institute of Health for osteoarthritis.

Mirror, Mirror on the Wall,
Can You Tell Me What You See

Diagnostic imaging such as x-rays may be ordered to examine the space between the vertebrae, the space through which nerve roots pass, and the space within the spinal canal. MRI (magnetic resonance imaging) is often used to confirm soft tissue abnormality such as disc protrusion, cartilage wear and ligament tears and CT scan (computed tomography) may be prescribed to visualize hard tissue abnormalities like bone cancer, spurs and fractures. Diagnostic imaging helps the integrative team of providers understand the extent of the osteoarthritis.

The Goals of Osteoarthritis Treatment

The goals of treating osteoarthritis are to manage pain, strengthen muscles of the affected area, restore range of motion and prevent further degeneration. Severe pain is often managed by the regulated use of analgesics and anti-inflammatory herbs, supplements and medication. Dull, chronic pain, however, can subside when strength and range of motion is restored. Acupuncture can relieve tension, reduce pain, restore blood circulation, reverse the energy crisis in the affected area and slow down the progression of osteoarthritis. Physical therapy can improve strength, restore range of motion and improve posture. Finally, osteoarthritis can be prevented or slowed down through proper posture, correct body mechanics during sports and everyday activities, consistent exercise that is restorative and appropriate for the individual, good diet and a healthy lifestyle.

Traction, Injections and Surgery

For osteoarthritis of the neck, cervical traction may be used. If pain still persists, corticosteroid (a highly potent anti-inflammatory) may be injected either into the tough membrane of the spinal cord or into the areas of the facet joints. These injections are used sparingly as they do have adverse effects if overused. For extremely severe osteoarthritis, surgery is the final option. Benefit from surgery, however, is not guaranteed. Furthermore, you must be aware of the risks of surgery before proceeding.

BULGING, HERNIATED AND RUPTURED DISC

Why You Want Your Discs to Be Plump

A disc in between two vertebrae has a gelatinous inner core and a fibrous outer shell. The disc provides flexibility of the vertebrae, absorbs mechanical shock from our daily activities and prevents bone-on-bone contact. The fibrous outer shell keeps the gelatinous inner core in its space. The outer core is made of collagen fibers, fat and water, giving it the ability to absorb fluid, elongate and recover continuously. While we are awake and active, body weight and muscle contractions are squeezing water out of the discs. While we are lying down asleep, water returns to the discs.

The younger you are, the more water you have in your discs relative to fat. This is why a younger person is noticeably taller in the morning than in the evening. As we age, the water content diminishes, the discs become thinner, and we become shorter. Three to 10 percent of disc fluid is lost from 10 hours of daily activity, but is recovered after at least 2 hours of rest. Prolonged tension in the muscles of the back can impede water recovery in the intervertebral discs.

Go Easy on Your Discs

Poor posture, weak core muscles, injured ligaments in the back, degenerated vertebrae, physical trauma to the back and pregnancy can also contribute to excessive pressure on intervertebral discs. Such stress on the discs can accelerate their degeneration. Degenerative discs often become noticeable around midlife (age 35 – 50) because they have lost a significant amount of water by this age and are more vulnerable to injury. Aggressive twisting of the back is especially compromising to the degenerative discs (especially twisting while bending over to lift). Extreme forward bending that is beyond your healthy range of motion also compromise the back and your intervertebral discs.

The Causes of Disc Tear

Excessive pressure on an intervertebral disc due to injury or accident can cause the outer fibrous shell (annulus fibrosus) to tear. If this tear does not result in a disc bulge or herniation, then it is referred to as simply an annular tear. The fibrous shell of the disc contains nerves that send pain signals to the brain when the shell is injured. But the pain of an annular tear stays localized in the lower back and is aggravated by positions and activities that add pressure to the compromised disc. For example, prolonged sitting will aggravate an annular tear. The pain, however, is alleviated by postures that relieve pressure on the injured disc, such as lying down.

Discography Is not a Style of Dance

A diagnostic procedure called a discography can confirm an annular tear. In this procedure, the suspect disc is injected with a fluid containing a dye. If the pain is triggered by the injection and the tear is visible through the dye and CT scan, then an annular tear is confirmed. This disc injury can usually be resolved through minimally invasive rehabilitation geared to reduce pain and correct imbalances in posture, relieving pressure on the disc over time.

Disorders of Discs Start With a Tear

The disc tear usually starts out microscopic, but can get worse as the gelatinous core continuously presses on it. As a result, the disc begins to bulge. At times, a bulge can progress to a herniation or rupture of the fibrous outer shell. This allows the gelatinous core to protrude further into either the spinal canal or the pathways between vertebrae which the nerve roots run through. The outer one-third of the fibrous shell of a disc contains nerves that are sensitive to pressure and sensitive to chemicals released through inflammatory response. Most of the time, these nerves are not negatively impacted by gradual disc degeneration through aging. In certain cases, however, degeneration can lead to pain. And sometimes, this pain originates within the nerves of the outer shell of the disc.

Chemicals That Cause More Pain

The protrusion of the disc into the spinal canal or into the intervertebral space causes irritation of surrounding ligaments and nerve tissue. Moreover, the injured disc releases chemicals such as prostaglandins, cytokines and others that send pain signals through sensory receptors to inform the brain of injury. These chemicals also trigger an inflammatory response within the surrounding ligaments, the sheath of the nerve roots (dural sheath) and the actual nerve roots. In summary, disc bulge and herniation irritate the nerve root by pressing on the nerve and releasing chemicals that trigger inflammation.

Radiculopathy Is Just Ridiculous

If the injured disc is located in the neck, symptoms usually include chronic neck pain. When the bulging or herniated disc irritates nerve roots and causes numbness, tingling and weakness of one arm or both arms, it is called radiculopathy. These symptoms can be more noticeable with certain movements or positions, and can vary in severity and frequency.

If the bulging or herniated disc is located in the lower back, symptoms usually include back pain that radiates down the buttock area and the leg, since nerve roots in the lower back can be irritated. The affected leg may also have numbness and weakness. This condition is known as sciatica, a form of radiculopathy. Whether or not symptoms are relieved or aggravated by standing and walking depends on which nerves are irritated.

Rest, acupuncture, therapeutic bodywork, anti-inflammatory herbs and anti-inflammatory foods can help to relieve symptoms due to injury of the intervertebral disc.

Healthy Blood Circulation Is Key to Back Healing

An injury to a disc will lead to inflammation and pain and will tighten surrounding soft tissue, especially muscle. These muscles will remain tight for several days, weeks or even months. This chronic tightness can apply excessive pressure on blood vessels, therefore obstructing the circulation of blood. Blood is essential for healing as it contains the nutrients and oxygen that enables tissue to regenerate. The circulation of blood is essential to removing toxins from the injured area.

Acupuncture relaxes tight muscles, reduces pressure on the blood vessels and restores blood flow to the site of the injury. Furthermore, acupuncture induces the release of the body's own anti-inflammatory chemicals to relieve stagnation and pain. As inflammation lessens and blood circulation is restored, the degeneration of the injured disc is slowed down. Acupuncture allows for the injured tissue to receive fresh nutrients and oxygen through blood flow. Acupuncture also improves circulation, flushing out toxins in the injured area. Therapeutic bodywork, anti-inflammatory herbs and foods help to support acupuncture in achieving relief.

Severe Disc Herniation
Requires Quick Medical Attention

In extreme cases of disc herniation, acupuncture may only provide temporary relief. If symptoms progress to loss of bladder or bowel control, the pain is not relieved by medication or loss of motor function and weakness is persistent, then the disc herniation could be severe and diagnostic imaging such as MRI may be required to evaluate the degree of the herniation. Rest, acupuncture, bodywork, herbs and diet may not be enough to resolve symptoms completely. A physician may prescribe painkillers, muscle relaxants and anti-inflammatories. Because of the side effects of these prescription drugs, one is not intended to be on them for the long term. The patient is reevaluated within a week if symptoms do not improve or if symptoms worsen.

Extreme Measures for an Extreme Condition

The next level of treatment for extreme disc herniation would be epidural steroid or nerve block injections along with physical therapy. If these procedures still do not provide relief, surgery may be considered to remove a piece of the herniated disc. Although most disc injuries are treated with non-surgical rehabilitation, surgery may be required for certain severe cases. Complete recovery from surgery, however, is not guaranteed. Furthermore, you must be aware of the risks of surgery before proceeding.

Once symptoms are relieved, however, a patient should strengthen his or her body through exercise and qi gong practices to prevent recurrence.

DEGNERATIVE DISC DISEASE

Don't Let Your Disc Dry Out

An intervertebral disc in the lower back can become increasingly deficient in fluid. This drying-up process can progress to the point that bones rub against one another, leading to irritation of the compromised disc and bone. Such irritation can trigger an inflammatory response and consequently a dull, chronic pain that is usually located either on one or both sides of the lower back. Sometimes this pain radiates into the buttock area. Pain is usually worse with bending forward forcefully, prolonged sitting and inactivity. Consequently, the pain is usually worse upon waking in the morning. There is usually less pain later in the day when there has been more movement throughout the day. Best prevention for dry discs: drink 6-8 glasses of water daily.

Take Pressure Off Your Discs With a Strong Core

People who have a disc injury are at higher risk of degenerative disc disease. A simple x-ray can confirm the diagnosis. You can prevent and relieve degenerative disc disease through exercises that lengthen and strengthen the core muscles, therefore relieve pressure on the degenerative disc. If you have degenerative disc disease, you should also avoid movements that go beyond your normal range of motion in the back. (See Chapter Six for core-strengthening exercises with Qi Gong for Back Health)

RADICULOPATHY

Radiculopathy Is a Pinched Nerve

A bulging or herniated disc can reduce the space between vertebrae through which nerve roots branch out of the spinal cord. Radiculopathy occurs when this space is obstructed to the point that nerve roots and their membranes (called dura) are irritated and inflamed. Other factors that can reduce intervertebral spaces include bone spurs, osteoarthritis and soft tissue injuries.

Symptoms of radiculopathy are pain, numbness, tingling and weakness in the affected area. For example, irritation of nerve roots in the neck can manifest as radiculopathy symptoms in the neck, shoulder, arm and hand. Irritation of nerve roots in the upper and middle back can manifest as symptoms in the upper and middle back. And irritation of nerve roots in the lower back can manifest in the lower back, buttock area, leg and foot.

Healing With Natural Medicine

Acupuncture, tuina bodywork, rehabilitative exercises, anti-inflammatory herbs and foods and other non-surgical modalities of care (such as chiropractic, osteopathy and traction) are most effective in relieving radiculopathy due to soft tissue injuries resulting to inflammation and nerve root impingement. As mentioned before, these non-invasive methods help to reduce inflammation, relieve tension, improve circulation and balance the nervous system.

The Last Resort Is Surgery

On the other hand, radiculopathy due to a more distinct structural obstruction of the intervertebral space (foramen) may call for a surgical procedure to achieve relief. Structural obstructions such as severe disc herniation and bone spurs from advanced osteoarthritis, for example, may require surgery. Again, you must be aware that complete resolution of pain is not guaranteed and that there are risks involved with surgery.

Even if you decide to undergo surgery, however, acupuncture, tuina bodywork, rehabilitative exercises, anti-inflammatory herbs and foods can still be of tremendous benefit throughout the post-surgical recovery phase.

SCIATICA

The Pain in Your Butt

The sciatic nerve is the longest and widest nerve of the human body. It innervates the skin of the leg and the muscles in the back of the leg. It begins in the lower back, travels down the buttock area, down the leg and through the sole of the foot. Its nerve roots branch out from the fourth lumbar vertebra through the third opening (foramen) in the sacrum. This bundle of nerve roots is referred to as the lumbosacral plexus.

Tracing the Sciatic Nerve

When the sciatic nerve is irritated, pain is felt along the anatomic path of the nerve and its branches. Pain may be felt through the lower back and buttock area. It may also be felt down the back of the leg and calf, above the lateral ankle and sometimes in areas of the foot. This pain is called sciatica. Sciatica is a type of radiculopathy, since it is caused by a compression of a nerve root as it exits the spine. Most of the time, sciatica is felt only in one side, but it can also be felt on both sides in certain cases. The pain can manifest in a variety of ways. Some report a heat sensation. Other times, the pain is a tingling sensation like an electrical current. Sometimes, the pain is severe and excruciating.

Why Is There Pain Shooting Down My Leg?

There are multiple causes of sciatica. As mentioned previously, a bulging or herniated disc is one cause for sciatica. Another cause is injured soft tissue that is inflamed and applying pressure on the sciatic nerve. Arthritis of the spine is another common cause. Excessive toxins in the body can also trigger sciatica. For example, toxins such as high levels of heavy metals or alcohol can trigger sciatica. At times, patients who are undergoing chemotherapy may also experience sciatica as a side effect. Systemic diseases such as diabetes can also leave you vulnerable to irritation of the sciatic nerve.

Chinese Medicine Comes to the Relief

The treatment of sciatica depends on the cause of this uncomfortable condition. Traditional Chinese medicine (acupuncture, tuina, herbal therapy, anti-inflammatory nutrition and restorative exercise) is effective in resolving sciatica caused by soft tissue injury. Acupuncture may be applied to specific areas along the pathway of the sciatic nerve, as well as clinically relevant points away from the affected area. Acupuncture not only reduces inflammation of the muscle irritating the sciatic nerve, but also reduces inflammation of the sciatic nerve itself and the nerves that branch out of it. When these nerves are less inflamed, then the muscles these nerves innervate will be less painful. As mentioned earlier, acupuncture achieves this pain relief by activating an anti-inflammatory reaction, allowing tense muscles to relax and improving the circulation of blood and lymphatic fluid.

An Integrative Approach for Optimum Benefit

As a rule, we advise patients to seek non-invasive, natural approaches to healing their back pain. If complete relief is not achieved through acupuncture, tuina, herbal therapy, anti-inflammatory nutrition, rehabilitative exercise and qi gong, then an orthopedic specialist, neurologist or physical therapist can be consulted for further medical evaluation. Nonetheless, traditional Chinese medicine can still be continued along with the modern modalities of medicine. An integrative approach will achieve optimum benefit for the patient.

PIRIFORMIS SYNDROME

There Is Another Muscle Under My Gluts

The piriformis is a muscle in the buttock area beneath the gluteus maximus. It starts at the lower spine, runs through the sacrum where the roots of the sciatic nerve are located and connects to the upper surface of the thigh bone (femur). The function of the piriformis is to help rotate the hip. Since hip rotation is an essential movement for walking, running and a large variety of other daily activities, the piriformis is extremely active.

Why Does My Butt Hurt?

Since the piriformis has such an important and demanding function to our daily lives, a weak piriformis can fatigue easily. Consequently, the fatigued piriformis is vulnerable to injury, inflammation and spasm. When the piriformis is inflamed and in spasm, it can generate pain when stretched and it can compress the root of the sciatic nerve. This leads to a sciatica-like symptom pattern: pain, numbness, tingling and weakness along the path of the sciatic nerve. This pain is felt in the buttock area, the leg and the foot of the affected side. The pain of piriformis syndrome is usually more severe while sitting than standing. The pain is also aggravated when you cross the affected leg over the other, because the injured piriformis is forced to stretch in this position. Furthermore, it is usually more noticeable upon waking if you sleep on your back. Moreover, hypersensitivity of a point close to the center of the buttock is a hallmark symptom of piriformis syndrome.

Since this is primarily a soft tissue injury, acupuncture, tuina, herbal therapy, anti-inflammatory nutrition, rehabilitative exercise and qi gong are very effective in relieving the spasm of the piriformis. The reduction of spasm reduces inflammation and pressure on the sciatic nerve roots. When the pressure is alleviated, the symptoms should be relieved.

SPINAL STENOSIS

When the Opening Narrows It Can Pinch a Nerve

The narrowing of the spinal column or the openings of the vertebrae is called spinal stenosis. Sometimes, the narrowing can irritate the spinal cord and trigger symptoms.

The narrowing may be caused by advanced osteoarthritis that has progressed to bone spurs. It may be caused by a birth defect or a tumor in the spine. And, as mentioned earlier, narrowing of the spinal column can also be caused by an injured disc or inflammation due to physical trauma. Spinal stenosis can also occur as a complication after a surgical procedure in the back, such as a laminectomy or fusion.

Narrowing Can Happen Anywhere on the Spine

There are people with spinal stenosis who do not feel symptoms. But others do. And when symptoms do occur, they typically worsen over time and manifest on one side of the body.

Symptoms of spinal stenosis in the lower back include tension and pain in the lower back, buttock and leg. The leg may also feel numb and weak. These symptoms worsen with standing and walking, but they lessen with sitting or leaning slightly forward. Symptoms of spinal stenosis in the neck include tension and pain in the neck, shoulders, arm and hand. The arm and hand may also feel numb and weak. Symptoms of severe spinal stenosis in the lower back that require immediate medical care include loss of balance and loss of bladder or bowel control.

A Physical Exam and Advanced Tests

Upon an office visit, a physical exam may be conducted to verify spinal stenosis. We may instruct you to walk on your toes and balls of the feet and then to walk on the heels. Then we ask you to bend your torso forward, backward and sideways. If you raise your legs straight up while lying down and report that your pain is worse, if sciatica occurs or if tingling and numbness occurs in one of the legs, we may suspect spinal stenosis. We may also perform a series of physical exams to check the strength of your legs and neurological function. We are likely to refer you for advanced tests such as EMG (electromyography), MRI, CT scan and x-ray, as well as a consult with a neurologist to verify or rule out spinal stenosis.

How Acupuncture Can Help Spinal Stenosis

Acupuncture can help relieve tension along the muscles that run bilaterally to the spine from the neck to the sacrum. These muscles are called erector spinae. By relieving tension in these muscles, acupuncture can increase blood circulation within the joints of the spine. Consequently, pressure on the nerve roots can be alleviated and inflammation of surrounding soft tissue in the affected area can be reduced. In conjunction with therapeutic bodywork like tuina, anti-inflammatory herbs and foods and rehabilitative exercises, acupuncture can be effective in achieving a certain level of relief from spinal stenosis.

When Other Structural Factors Are Present

More invasive modalities such as prescription medication, steroid and analgesic injections and even surgery (i.e. foraminotomy, laminectomy, and spinal fusion) may be considered for more severe spinal stenosis that stems from structural factors such as bone spurs. Even in these cases, acupuncture can still be integrated with the more aggressive therapies to reduce pain and to promote rehabilitation. Drastic surgery may either partially or completely relieve symptoms. Yet, sustained relief after surgery is not guaranteed. Another point to consider is that the back is likely to have more problems in the future if appropriate lifestyle choices are not made after surgery.

BRUISED BACK

A Bruised Back Happens When You Get Hit or Fall Down

Bruises of the back are usually caused by blunt force trauma to the middle and lower back. Such trauma may occur from a fall or from participation in full contact sports such as hockey, American football, rugby, martial arts, wrestling and boxing. The impact of a blunt force trauma on soft tissue such as muscle, tendon and ligament can cause a rupture of its cells. Such an injury will usually manifest as pain that worsens after a few days. This pain is usually very localized and may be detectable by a discoloration of red, purple, black and blue.

Simple Remedies to Hasten Healing

Bruises can be treated with a simple application of ice wrapped in cloth to protect the skin from ice burn. The ice should be applied for no more than 20 minutes at a time. Over the counter anti-inflammatory medication may be used for a brief duration if you do not have gastrointestinal sensitivity. Anti-inflammatory and circulatory herbs and foods such as tumeric and pineapple can be beneficial for treating bruises with less possibility for gastrointestinal side effects. Bruises should improve within a few days. If not, you should consult with a medical physician. Diagnostic imaging may be ordered to rule out a more serious injury such as a broken bone or organ damage.

SACROILIAC JOINT INJURY

What Joins Your Back and Pelvis Together

As mentioned in chapter one, the pelvic girdle (where the sacrum joins the hip) is the foundation of the spine. The two joints that connect the sacrum with the two iliac bones of the pelvis are called the sacroiliac or SI joints. Since these joints are located at the foundation of the spine, they must be somewhat pliable while we carry out a variety of movements throughout our days. But when these joints bear weight, they tighten to keep the pelvic girdle stable. The angle of the pelvic tilt is a primary factor to the health of these joints as well as to the health of the entire spine, since it is this tilt that determines posture.

SI Joints Hold Your Weight Above the Waist

The sacrum is the root of the spine. As the root, the sacrum and the sacroiliac joints support the entire weight of the body above the waist. Common activities such as lifting, pulling, pushing, bending, walking, running and twisting put stress on the sacroiliac joint. The surfaces of the sacroiliac joint consist of many notches and tabs that must fit into one another very precisely. This joint is stabilized by ligaments that only move by a few millimeters in order to be pliable enough for daily activities, while maintaining the perfect fit of the joint surfaces. Because the sacroiliac joints support the entire weight above the waist, they are susceptible to injury. And injuries to the sacroiliac joints can generate pain.

When Pain Is Worse Getting Out of Bed or Your Car

Symptoms of sacroiliac joint injury include pain or tenderness in the areas of the sacroiliac joint, the pelvis, and the upper buttock. Pain may also be felt along the pathway of the sciatic nerve, radiating down to the lower buttock and the leg of the affected side. Pain is usually worse when lifting the leg of the affected side and when putting weight on that leg. This pain may be especially noticeable when getting out of bed or out of a car. Sometimes, the pain is also felt when twisting the back. The pain is sometimes worse when bending forward from the waist with the legs straight. Pain is also usually worse with prolonged sitting or standing.

Why SI Joints Get Injured

A common cause of this injury is an imbalanced tonicity of muscles attached to the pelvis. Such an imbalance can pull this joint out of alignment. Another possible cause is an injury of the ligament that keeps the sacroiliac joint together. Sacroiliac joint injury can also be brought on by a fracture of either the sacrum or the pelvis. Pregnancy or rapid weight gain may also leave you vulnerable to this injury. Aggressive twisting movements can also cause sacroiliac joint injury. Participation in activities that involve high impact in the lower back, such as ballet, modern dance, gymnastics and basketball, also increase your risk.

SI Joint Injury Cannot Be Diagnosed with Imaging Tests

Sacroiliac joint injury usually does not show up in diagnostic tools such as x-rays, MRIs, or electromyography. A physical exam by a qualified health care provider is typically how this injury is diagnosed. The definitive test, however, is the injection of a nerve block into the affected joint. If temporary cessation of pain results from the injection, then sacroiliac joint injury is confirmed.

What to Do After Injury

Upon injury of the sacroiliac joint, you should rest and avoid aggravating activities that put excessive stress on the injured joint. Continuing to play sports with this injury can prolong healing time. A special belt that wraps around the hips can be worn to squeeze the sacrum to the pelvis and help stabilize the joint while it is injured. For severe pain, you may be prescribed pharmaceutical anti-inflammatory medication or even painkillers, but only very temporarily because of the possible side effects of such drugs.

Healing With Chinese Medicine and Non-Invasive Therapies

Acupuncture, tuina bodywork, anti-inflammatory foods and anti-inflammatory herbs can also be utilized to ease the pain, reduce inflammation and improve circulation in the injured area. Acupuncture is especially effective in reducing pain, relaxing the affected muscles and improving regional blood supply, thus helping recovery of the soft tissues near the injured sacroiliac joint.

Once the tightness of the soft tissue has been relieved, a physical therapist, chiropractor, osteopath or qualified tuina bodywork practitioner can gently mobilize the affected joint to restore its function. Specific rehabilitative exercise can be incorporated under the guidance of a physical therapist to restore the pliability of the muscles attached to the pelvis. The physical therapist may also incorporate strengthening exercises for the abdomen, the lower back, the legs and pelvic floor to reduce excessive stress on the sacroiliac joint.

FACET JOINT SYNDROME

The Lego Pieces of the Vertebrae

As mentioned in chapter one, facet joints are the connections for the backbones. These connections allow the backbones to be stacked above one another as the facet joints run in pairs down the entire spine. They help stabilize the spine by preventing excessive movement that may compromise the spinal cord. Each facet joint is lined with cartilage and is surrounded by a lubricated capsule that allows the spine to bend and twist.

When facet joints are stressed and injured, facet joint syndrome can occur. This can be caused by an injury of the back, degeneration of an intervertebral disc, or from everyday wear and tear. The cartilage covering the facet joint gradually wears away and the joint swells and stiffens. The wearing away of the cartilage can become so severe that the vertebral bones rub against one another which increases the probability of bone spurs developing along the edges of the facet joints.

When the Lego Coupling Gets Damaged

The location and symptoms of facet joint syndrome pain depends on which facet joints are damaged. For example, if a facet joint is damaged in the neck, pain may be felt in the neck, shoulders, upper back and middle back. Headaches may also occur as a result of facet joint syndrome in the neck. On the other hand, a damaged facet joint in the lower back can lead to pain in the lower back, the buttocks and in the back of the thigh.

Take it Easy With Hot and Cold

During painful episodes of facet joint syndrome, you should avoid all activities that trigger pain. You may also apply ice on the affected area in the first two days following injury. Place a cloth on the skin where the ice is applied to prevent ice burn. Icing should not exceed 20 minutes at a time. After the initial two days, you should switch to using a heating pad at medium setting for 20 minutes two to three times a day. Mild to moderate use of analgesics and anti-inflammatory medication may be used for severe pain (keeping in mind that excessive use of such medications may have adverse effects).

Healing With Chinese Medicine and Natural, Non-Invasive Therapies

Acupuncture can promote the release of tension, the increase of blood circulation and the release of pain-reducing endorphins. Muscles, nerves, tendons and ligaments can become less inflamed and consequently more capable of healing. Maintaining a healthy back may slow down the degeneration of the facet joints.

Manual therapies such as tuina bodywork, chiropractic and osteopathy may also be helpful in reducing facet joint syndrome pain. Rehabilitative exercises that are focused on strengthening the core and lengthening the hamstrings may also be effective in relieving and reducing pain. Such exercises help prevent hyperextension of the back that compromises the facet joints. Physiotherapy such as ultrasound and moist heat can also help to control pain.

Through the integration of acupuncture, manual therapies, physiotherapy, rehabilitative exercise and anti-inflammatory foods and herbs you can reduce facet joint syndrome pain. Reducing the risk of recurrence of such pain is also important. You can protect the back from further degeneration by continuing the treatments and exercises on a regular basis.

Healing and Prevention With Herbal, Nutritional and Acupuncture Therapies

Anti-inflammatory herbs such as turmeric, myrrh and frankincense and foods such as papaya, pineapple and kiwi may also help to reduce inflammation, improve circulation, reduce pain and restore strength. As we age, a normal level of wear and tear on the facet joints is inevitable. Regular acupuncture treatments can help you to develop healthy and strong muscles along the spine, with optimized blood circulation. The nutrients and oxygen transported by the blood can slow down degeneration and keep you active and healthy into your old age.

For facet joint syndrome that is not sufficiently relieved by non-invasive approaches, fluoroscopic-guided facet joint injection of anti-inflammatory and nerve blocking analgesics may be an option.

SPONDYLOLISTHESIS

When Vertebrae Slippage Happens

In this condition, injury of bones or joints causes a vertebra to slip forward. This forward slippage will usually occur at the fourth lumbar vertebra or at the fifth lumbar vertebra. Such a slippage can affect the spinal cord and pinch nerves, leading to dull ache in the lower back, radiating pain in the buttocks and pain that can radiate down the leg and foot of the affected side. Pain is usually worse with extension.

Two Causes of Vertebrae Slippage

There are multiple causes for spondylolisthesis, but two causes tend to be more common—degenerative and isthmic. Degenerative spondylolisthesis occurs when the joints weaken, allowing a vertebra to slip forward. As nerve roots become pinched, pain will often radiate down the leg and foot. Isthmic spondylolisthesis occurs when the vertebral bone fractures, allowing a vertebra to slip forward. This slippage can also pinch nerve roots causing pain to radiate to the leg and foot.

Detection With a Simple X-Ray

Spondylolisthesis can usually be detected through x-ray. The severity of the condition is graded from I through IV. In the initial phase of injury, you may wear a brace to prevent excessive extension of the back. Protecting the back from hyperextension is intended to prevent the injury on the affected vertebra from getting worse. Method and duration of treatment depends on the severity of the slippage.

When Spondylolisthesis Becomes Chronic

Individuals who have had spondylolisthesis for a long time may be vulnerable to recurring and chronic pain. Acupuncture, anti-inflammatory foods and anti-inflammatory herbs that promote circulation may be helpful in managing this pain. If pain persists, anti-inflammatory medication, muscle relaxants and painkillers may be prescribed by a medical doctor, but only for short term use to avoid chemical dependency and side effects. Physical therapy for spondylolisthesis is focused on core stabilization, pelvic floor strengthening and biomechanics.

Chapter Three

Activate Your Engery Channels: Benefits of Acupuncture and Bodywork for Back Pain

Acupuncture and tuina bodywork have been in continuous use for thousands of years as an integral part of Chinese medicine. These techniques have been used by billions of people in China, Japan, Korea, Vietnam, many parts of Asia and in the last 40 years, in many countries of Europe and the U.S. The ancient premise is that there are channels networked throughout the human body filled with vital life force or "qi" energy (pronounced "chee"). Qi is understood as both informational and substance of nourishment. It allows for communication between the body and the mind and is responsible for all aspects of the human biological function. Blockage of qi flow is the cause of illness and pain. Removal of stagnation and restoration of qi flow is the goal of acupuncture and tuina bodywork.

Acupuncture is very effective in relieving neck and back pain and works by stimulating the body's self-healing mechanism. It involves the insertion of hair-thin needles into the skin, which stimulates sensory nerves to send signals through the peripheral and central nervous systems, consequently affecting three important factors to healing: the physiological healing process, homeostasis (the body's tendency to restore functional balance) and the holistic nature of the human being (the interrelationship of physical, emotional and mental aspects).

To understand the efficacy of acupuncture, we must first understand the most fundamental aspects of the human nervous system. Structurally, the nervous system is comprised of the central nervous system and the peripheral nervous system. The central nervous system is the brain and spinal cord, and the peripheral nervous system is everything else. In the following pages you will learn how acupuncture helps to facilitate healing and relieve pain.

Acupuncture Removes Blockages to Self-Healing

In ancient China, people observed the phenomenon of a universal life energy they called qi (pronounced "chee") that circulated throughout every living thing along pathways in the body. Health was maintained if this energy flowed freely, but when the pathways were blocked and the qi no longer flowed smoothly, it resulted in pain and disease. Imagine body fluids stagnating like a swamp or the nervous system short-circuiting; these are symptoms of qi blockages.

Acupuncture was invented more than five millennia ago to address these blockages and guide your body back to doing what it does best. The art of acupuncture is in the placement of fine needles along defined pathways, stimulating a focused response from the nervous, cardiovascular, musculoskeletal, hormonal and immune systems, restoring qi movement and bringing balance and harmony back to the body. Back pain and inflammation respond well to acupuncture and many studies have confirmed its efficacy. You can expect an average case of back pain to improve after only a few treatments. But if the condition is more severe or long-lasting, it may take a longer course of treatments, more than 10 or 12, before progress can be noticed.

Acupuncture Closes the Gate on Pain

Acupuncture relieves back pain by sending signals through the nervous system to the brain. These healing signals calm signals sent by pain receptors located around the injured area. In a neurological sense, acupuncture closes the gate on pain. In 1965, Dr. Ronald Melzack and Dr. Patrick Wall proposed that pain signals travel to the brain through fine nerve fibers. These pain signals, however, are controlled and modified in the spinal cord by signals traveling through the large nerve fibers that reach the brain before the pain signal does. Acupuncture is effective in blocking some of the painful stimuli reaching the brain, therefore altering the mental experience of pain. This period of pain relief serves as a "window of opportunity" for the back pain sufferer to induce a relaxation response that is essential to healing.

Acupuncture Induces Endorphin Release

Acupuncture is recognized by the National Institute of Health (NIH) as an effective modality to induce the release of endorphins, which help the back pain sufferer experience significant pain relief. In the early 1970s, it was discovered that the human brain makes its own natural, pain relieving opioid peptide compounds or "endogenous morphine," hence the name of this natural pain reliever, endorphin. Four types of endorphins have been identified: beta-endorphin, encephalin, dynorphin and endomorphin. Endorphin (endogenous morphine or opioid polypeptide compound) is created by your own body (more specifically your pituitary gland and hypothalamus, an area of the brain) to relieve pain and stress, promote a sense of well-being and help the back pain sufferer to enter a calm state of mind that is conducive to healing.

Acupuncture Activates An Anti-Inflammatory Response

Acupuncture helps heal back pain by enhancing the brain's response to injury. The signals sent through the vast nervous system activates the brain's self-healing mechanism and optimizes the release of anti-inflammatory compounds created by your body and delivered to the site of injury. Acupuncture also initiates the relaxation response, which sets the stage for restoration of damaged tissue and physiological control systems that have been disrupted by injury.

Acupuncture Improves Circulation

Acupuncture can improve circulation by dilating the smooth muscles of the blood vessels, thereby increasing blood flow in and out of the affected site, enhancing nutrient delivery and eliminating waste and toxins. Acupuncture also has the ability to relax chronic muscle contractions. Consequently, this ancient modality helps to balance muscular tone and elasticity and facilitate the healing of damaged tissue. Acupuncture is utilized for all regions of the back, from the neck to the thoracic mid-back region to the lower back and finally to the sacrum.

Qi is the Force that Brings Living Tissue to Life

In the context of traditional Chinese medicine, acupuncture is intended to balance bioelectric energy referred to as qi. This bioelectric energy is believed to be the force that brings living tissue to life. In fact, observation of the state of this energy is a primary factor in determining the diagnosis. Imbalance in this bioelectric energy implies disease or injury. Acupuncture attempts to correct and prevent the imbalance by supporting the self-healing and self-regulating mechanisms of the individual.

Electric Current + Acupuncture = Electroacupuncture

Electroacupuncture (EA) works by attaching a battery-powered electrical current to the acupuncture needle to depolarize nerve endings, consequently activating cell-to-cell communication and enhancing nerve impulses to the brain through the spinal cord. It can also enhance pain-blocking signals to the brain. The frequency of the electrical stimulation determines the type of endorphins released. Electrical stimulation through acupuncture needles can also induce the release of other neurochemical pain relievers such as serotonin and norepinephrine. EA enhances systemic and local blood circulation. The improved circulation relaxes muscle and improves healing.

Bodywork Encompasses More Than Just Massage

Tuina (pronounced "twee-na") is a highly evolved system of bodywork that applies the fundamental principles of Chinese medicine, which is to restore harmonious flow of qi energy and blood through the body's system of energetic pathways and blood vessels, facilitating healing. Tuina is extremely effective in relieving back pain in that it encompasses a broad range of bodywork techniques, including massage, deep tissue release, joint mobilization, cupping and gua sha techniques.

Some of the unique techniques of tuina include stroking, kneading, pressing, traction, percussion, friction, pulling, rotating, rocking, vibration and shaking. Tuina focuses achieving therapeutic effect rather than just relaxation and has long been used by Chinese Olympic athletes for both rehabilitation and prevention of injury. Olympic athletes from the U.S. and other countries are increasingly incorporating aspects of tuina as part of their training regimen.

Tuina serves as an effective complement to other modalities of Chinese Medicine such as acupuncture and herbal therapy.

Cupping Grabs Attention at the Rio Olympic Games

When the U.S. Olympic swim team members, including Michael Phelps, prepared for the Rio Games, they revealed round markings on their backs. The mysterious markings were from cupping, a healing modality that's long been part of tuina bodywork. Cupping induces suction achieved by placing round, glass jars on the skin immediately after burning out the oxygen from inside the jar or a suction instrument. The suction from cupping quickly increases circulation to the affected muscle tissue, pulling the toxins to the surface to be eliminated and supplying critical nutrients for healing. Cupping also stretches the muscle fiber, therefore countering muscle spasms and contractions. It can quickly relief soreness and pain after an athletic strain.

Self-Care With Acupressure

Acupressure is a healing technique that involves applying manual pressure to specific acupoints on the body for therapeutic effect. It is sometimes called acupuncture without needles. However, it does not replace acupuncture—a medical procedure with profound therapeutic outcomes. Instead acupressure is a wonderful complement to other modalities within Chinese medicine. By activating acupoints located on specific channels through your body, you can increase circulation, release tension and reduce pain in your neck and back. Acupressure is simple to learn and easy to do. Pressure should be applied gradually according to comfort level. You do not need to push hard on the point to achieve effectiveness. Gently visualizing the pain melting away or moving your painful areas while you perform acupressure can also be effective.

In the following pages, we have provided several acupressure points to help you relieve pain and help unblock your channels and vessels for health and healing.

Balance the Core with Wei Zhong (B40)

The name of this acupoint is literally "Balance the Core." As its name implies, traditionally it has been used for abdominal weakness leading to lower back pain and weakness. It is located behind the knees, at the midpoint of the crease behind the knees, between two large tendons. Apply gentle but steady pressure to this point with your finger to relieve muscle spasm and pain and to help unblock the bladder channel, which traverses the back on both sides of the spine. Hold steady pressure for one minute, release pressure for 30 seconds and continue to alternate between pressure and release for 10 minutes and then repeat the same on the other knee.

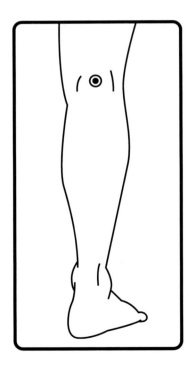

Relieve Lumbar Pain with Yao Tong

The name of this acupoint is literally "lumbar pain." It is actually a pair of acupoints located on the back side of the hands, one between the second and third metacarpal or hand bones and the other between the fourth and fifth metacarpal bones. You can slide a finger from the fingers along the back of the hand towards the wrist, in the groove between the metacarpal bones until you reach the tender spot close to where the metacarpals or hand bones join together. Hold pressure steady for one minute, release pressure for 30 seconds and continue to alternate between pressure and release for 10 minutes and then repeat the same on the other hand.

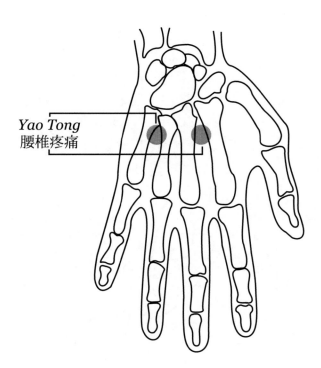

Yao Tong
腰椎疼痛

Calm Spirit and Strengthen Bones With Ling Gu

The name of this acupoint is literally "spirit and bones" and it has traditionally been used to relieve pain that is caused by stress and trauma. Ling Gu activates qi and blood flow and and is located between the first and second metacarpal or hand bones. The acupoint is found at the v-junction between these bones. Apply steady and firm pressure so as to experience tenderness at the v-junction for one minute, release pressure for 30 seconds and continue to alternate between pressure and release for 10 minutes and then repeat the same on the other hand. You may find that the hand on the opposite side of the pain tends to be more tender and effective.

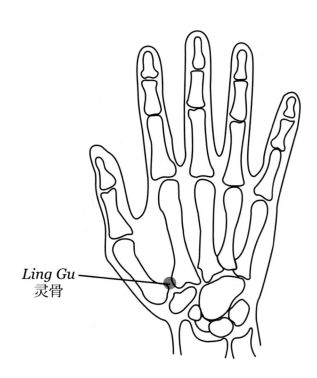

Ling Gu
灵骨

Relieve Spine Disorders With Kun Lun (B60)

The name of this acupoint means "Himalayan mountains." It is found between the Achille's tendon and the outside of the ankle bone. It has traditionally been used for vertebrae or disc problems as well as for muscle spams and pinched nerves like sciatica. Find tenderness and press on the acupoint while mobilizing your neck or the portion of your back that hurts.

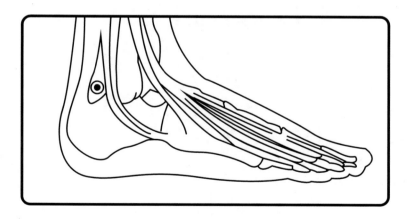

Clear the Back Channels With Hou Xi (SI 3)

The name of this acupoint means "back stream" and it has traditionally been used for activating energy and fluid flow in the governing channel which runs down the spine. This acupoint is located in the ulnar or underside of your hand, in the indentation just below the head of your fifth metacarpal hand bone. It is easier to locate when the hand is made into a loose fist. Stimulate this acupoint to activate the spine, regulate nerve conduction and reduce pain.

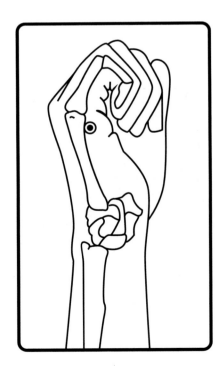

Other Home Healing Remedies and Apparatuses

Essential oils, such as those found in Tonic Oil (available at wellnesslivingstore.com)—including eucalyptus, wintergreen, mint, fennel, cinnamon and ginger—can bring temporary relief when you massage them on your muscles and areas of pain. The results are often immediate. Apply Tonic Oil on your neck, back or painful joints before bedtime and use a heating pad over the area for 20 minutes to help you ease pain and sleep better.

In addition to the acupoints listed above, any sensitive points on the body where there is a tightness, a contraction or knot in the skeletal muscle, can lead to a stagnation of blood circulation in the local tissue and potentially cause referred pain in another part of the body. Use of manual therapy tools such as foam rollers, tennis/lacrosse balls or Theracane can be beneficial for home use. Ask your health practitioner which of these might be right for you and get instruction to use them properly.

Chapter Four

Eat Right to Heal Right:
Nutrition and Herbal Therapy

Having proper nutrition is key to health and healing. Eating therapeutically can help you reduce pain, promote circulation, reduce inflammation and heal the muscles of the back. Eating a well-balanced diet with a variety of vegetables, fruits, lean proteins and whole grains will give your muscular-skeletal structure the basic building blocks it needs. As your body is nourished, your overall energy will improve, allowing your body to be more efficient in its self-healing.

Chinese dietary and nutritional therapy can be encapsulated in one word: balance. Your body is always aiming for homeostasis. Chinese dietary and nutritional therapy takes into consideration where the imbalances are in your body and aims to correct the root cause of illness. If you are suffering from swelling and inflammation, our certified nutrition experts will recommend foods that cool the inflammation, reduce swelling and increase healing, which in turn will calm the nervous system and reduce pain.

Nutritional supplements play an important role in health and healing. Over the last 50 years, industrialized farming techniques have depleted the soil of essential nutrients, and changes in the microbiome have affected the way nutrients are absorbed and utilized in our body. Studies comparing nutrient contents of 43 different vegetables and fruits from 1950 and 1999 found "reliable declines" in the amount of protein, calcium, phosphorus, iron, riboflavin (vitamin B2) and vitamin C over the past half century. Another study saw the average calcium levels in 12 fresh vegetables dropped 27 percent, iron levels 37 percent, vitamin A levels 21 percent and vitamin C levels 30 percent. The sad fact is that you would have to eat eight oranges today to derive the same amount of beta-carotene (Vitamin A) as your grandparents would have gotten from one.

Deficiencies of certain nutrients can lead to increased risks for disease. For instance, the majority of the U.S. women are deficient in vitamin D which is essential in hormonal function and the health of bones. Vitamin D deficiency has been shown to correlate with increased incidence of certain cancers, including breast cancer, as well as osteoporosis which can lead to back pain. Deficiencies can also come from causes other than soil nutrient depletion. For example, statin drugs are the most popularly prescribed drugs for high cholesterol. One of its side effects is blocking the production of the enzyme Co-Q10 which acts as an anti-oxidant that repairs muscle tissue. The resulting low levels of Co-Q10 in people taking statin drugs have contributed to muscle pain, and in rare cases, muscle wasting. Supplementing with Co-Q10 in these patients is the obvious answer to preventing the side effects of statin drugs.

Discussions on diet and nutrition is incomplete without Chinese herbal therapy. Herbs have long been part of a health-promoting, disease prevention diet and lifestyle program in China and many cultures around the world. Oregano, rosemary, thyme, parsley, sage, coriander, ginger, turmeric, fennel and many other herbs are commonly found in everyday meals around the world. These and other herbs possess potent therapeutic properties that when used in a targeted fashion can improve healing from illness and reduce inflammation and pain.

In addition to the edible herbs above, medicinal herbs are traditionally made into tea and used for healing. Herbal therapy has been time-tested for thousands of years in China and throughout the world and has little or no side effects. However, it's important that you consult a licensed acupuncturist and doctor of Chinese medicine to obtain expert advice in customizing herbal therapy for your condition.

Chinese Herbal Therapy

When treating back pain, the focus of an expert practitioner of Chinese herbal therapy is to activate blood flow and reduce inflammation. When a back injury occurs, blood vessels may be damaged along with muscle, tendon and ligament. The result is inflammation that may aggravate the nerves and stagnate blood and body fluid. When soft tissue and blood vessels are damaged through traumatic injury of the back, body fluids may leak out of the blood and lymphatic vessels and become trapped in the interstitial layers. The consequence is inflammation and swelling of the injured area.

During the acute stage of injury, inflammation can immobilize the joint and prevent further injury, but if stagnation continues beyond the acute stage, it becomes an obstacle to the healing process. Such inflammation can restrict the range of motion of the affected joints, restrict the flow of blood and nerve signals and irritate pain receptors. Herbal therapy for back pain intends to restore circulation. When the circulation of blood is optimized, healing is optimized, for blood transport nutrients and oxygen to injured tissue that is essential for healing.

Herbal and botanical substances can be a powerful part of a therapeutic protocol for neck and back pain. Herbs, whether Chinese or Western, should be used according to individual need. We highly recommend you seek guidance and customized formulation from a licensed practitioner, as some herbal supplements may interact with drug medications. For example, ginkgo biloba can exaggerate the anticoagulant effect of Warfarin and other blood thinners, and garlic does the same with the platelet-inhibiting drug Tiplopidine.

As a general rule, avoid taking prescription medication within 30 minutes of taking herbs or supplements. As your health strategies change and evolve, do not stop taking prescription medications without first speaking to your physician.

In the following pages you will find a list of foods, nutritional supplements and herbs that possess special properties to fight inflammation, improve blood circulation and activate the body's healing response. Just as important, you will also find a list of foods to avoid as they are pro-inflammatory and will aggravate your condition. The listed herbs can be taken by themselves in a tea, capsule or in combination with other herbs as formulated by a licensed practitioner.

Top 10 Anti-Inflammatory Healing Foods

Papaya

Inflammation in the body resembles fire in its destructive power. Recent research strongly indicates that inflammation is the root of all degenerative diseases, including heart disease, arthritis, Alzheimer's, Parkinson's and senility. The most severe of these conditions are incurable and fatal. But nature's inflammation fighter comes to the rescue. Papaya contains papain, an enzyme found to help reduce pain, inflammation and fluid retention following trauma and surgery. In fact, studies have shown that papain possesses marked anti-inflammatory activity, and this ability is no less than that of the pharmaceutical drug indomethacin, without the side effects.

Pineapple

Pineapple contains enzymes called bromelain that have been used by Europeans for many years to inhibit inflammation. Bromelain has been found to reduce the inflammatory process, modulate overactive immune responses and relieve allergies. Studies have shown that bromelain's anti-inflammatory properties come from its ability to effectively inhibit neutrophil, part of the immune system troops. As a result, it can be helpful in reducing swelling and speeding up the healing of surgical wounds, sprains and bruises. So before you resort to an anti-inflammatory drug, try eating a big bowl of pineapple!

Grapes

Extensive research has confirmed the benefits of grapes due to their high content of the antioxidant resveratrol. This compound, found in the skin of grapes, possesses anti-inflammatory properties and can reduce cholesterol and prevent cancer. Grapes also keep the blood from thickening in the blood vessels—preventing blood clots, stroke and plaque buildup. Grapeseed is the actual star as it contains a compound called oligomeric proanthocyanidin complexes (OPCs). OPCs are most well known for their antioxidant activity and have been found effective in reducing swelling and nerve pain.

Cherries

Chinese doctors have long observed that cherries help keep joints and muscles healthy. The antioxidant anthocyanins that impart the dark pigments to cherries, grapes and berries have been found to reduce inflammation and ease muscle pain. Studies also show that consuming up to three servings of cherries in two days can lead to a 50% reduction in risk of gout. Those who drank tart cherry juice twice daily for three weeks had significant reductions in markers of inflammation. They also had a 20 percent reduction in pain. Finally, athletes who consumed tart cherry juice prior to long-distance running experienced less pain than those who did not.

Fish

Certain fish are good sources of omega-3 fatty acids, which have been found to fight inflammation. Studies show that people with the highest consumption of omega-3s had lower levels of interleukin-6 and C-reactive protein (CRP). Moreover, those with back pain and rheumatoid arthritis who took fish oil supplements experienced reduced pain, joint swelling and morning stiffness. The fish with the highest omega-3 fatty acids include salmon, arctic char, black cod, mackerel, scallops and sardines.

Walnuts

Walnuts have been prized for centuries as both a food and herb, and are the richest source of omega-3 fatty acids among all nuts. They were traditionally used as a brain and heart tonic and now studies have confirmed that walnuts are rich in ellagic acid, which possesses anti-atherogenic properties—meaning it prevents plaque from forming and hardening arteries. Due to their high arginine content, walnuts may increase circulation by dilating blood vessels. When it comes to pain relief, the fatty acids in walnuts inhibit the production of neurotransmitters such as substance P and bradykinins, which increase pain and inflammation. As an added bonus, studies found that over a 15-year period men and women who consumed the most nuts, including walnuts, had a 51 percent lower risk of dying from an inflammatory disease such as rheumatoid arthritis compared with those who ate the fewest nuts. Who knew this brain-shaped nut packs such a big punch when it comes to health benefits!

Turmeric

Turmeric is a popular cooking spice, found in curry, that comes from the curcuma plant in the ginger family. It is native to tropical South Asia and has been used in traditional medicines for the treatment of sprains, strains, bruises and inflammation of the joints. Many studies have been conducted on turmeric and have found it to possess anti-inflammatory and anti-cancer properties. This spice is used primarily for pain, particularly from traumatic injury, as well as pain in the chest, flanks, abdomen or discomfort related to menstruation. Turmeric can be found fresh in some stores' produce sections and is available as a powder, as a chopped and dried herb, and as a tea, tincture, oil or in capsules. You will surely want to add the spice to your cooking to promote healthy circulation.

Ginger

Ginger has a long history, dating back several thousand years in China, of providing both culinary and medicinal use for pain in the muscles and joints. Modern research has discovered that it possesses anti-inflammatory properties. One of the therapeutic ingredients, gingerols, as well as other active compounds, have been shown to suppress pro-inflammatory factors such as cytokines and chemokines and prevent free-radical damage to the muscle and joint tissue. Ginger has even been shown to work better than drugs for arthritic knees. In a study of patients with rheumatoid arthritis, osteoarthritis and muscular discomfort, the majority of those who received ginger experienced relief of pain and swelling. Include as much ginger in your diet plan as possible; add ginger to your dishes, make a tea out of fresh ginger root and take it in capsule form as well.

Cayenne

Throughout the ages, chili peppers have been used for pain relief. In Chinese medicine, cayenne has been used to increase blood circulation, "warm up" your body's interior, relieve pain and open up the channels. The powerful heat in cayenne peppers comes from capsaicin, which not only gives food a spicy kick but also fights inflammation. Research shows that it has proven effective in healing pain associated with arthritis, back pain and nerve pain. Capsaicin cream is usually used to relieve pain and itching topically. Though its ability to reduce a pain-transmitting neurochemical is most effective when applied to the skin, capsaicin can also be helpful for easing joint stiffness and relieving sore muscles. However, you may want to skip this particular pepper if you have red, burning pain in your muscles or joints or if you experience heartburn or indigestion. Cayenne and capsaicin are also available in capsule form.

Rosemary

Carnosol, a compound found in rosemary, has been shown to inhibit COX-2 activities. There are two types of enzymes prevalent in the human body called cyclo-oxygenase (COX), or COX-1 and COX-2. The COX-1 enzyme is found in most tissues and is involved in protecting the stomach lining, ensuring kidney health and encouraging proper clotting. The COX-2 enzyme, on the other hand, is a critical component of the inflammation process, but when inflammation gets out of control and results in arthritis or other chronic inflammatory disorders, pain is the consequence. Drugs like Celebrex are prescribed to block COX-2 but have unpleasant side effects. That's where natural COX-2 inhibitors such as rosemary are preferable, because they can help without the side effects.

Tea

For thousands of years, tea has been used as a healing agent by cultures around the world. White, red, green and black tea all come from the same camellia sinensis tea plant, which originated in China. Green tea is among the most potent sources of antioxidants and includes epigallocatechin gallate (EGCG), a powerful catechin substance that inhibits the activity of cartilage-destroying enzymes. Black tea contains quercetin, a bioflavanoid that has been shown to play a role in relieving the inflammation associated with rheumatoid arthritis and preventing joint damage. With all these benefits what are you waiting for? Switch from coffee to tea and your back will thank you for it!

Top 10 Inflammation-Inducing Foods to Avoid

Night Shades: Potato, Tomato, Eggplant, Bell Pepper

Chinese medicine views many types of pain as inflammation, and eating certain common foods can be like adding fuel to the fire, making inflammatory pain worse. The nightshade family of vegetables can stimulate an inflammatory reaction in the body when you eat them. Nightshades include potatoes, tomatoes, eggplant and bell peppers. Its most famous cousin, belladonna, is a highly toxic plant that was thought to be responsible for several mysterious deaths in medieval Europe. Modern research has discovered the culprit—solanine, an alkaloid that irritates the immune system and leads to the inflammatory response. Clinically, we've found that small amounts of these foods are tolerated by patients with mild cases of back pain or arthritis. This includes a few pieces of sun-dried tomatoes, a couple small potatoes, or a slice or two of eggplant. One study showed that lutein, an antioxidant found in tomatoes, might protect against osteoarthritis. However, during active disease flare-ups it is advisable to stay away from nightshades completely.

Sugar and Refined Carbohydrates

Sugar in its natural form is the food that each of our cells requires for production of ATP. ATP stands for adenosine triphosphate, and it is the energy our cells release that allows our bodies to function properly. In whole foods that contain natural sugars such as fruits, vegetables and whole grains, the sugars are bound to the whole food's protein or fiber, essentially time releasing the sugar into your bloodstream. This helps to avoid an excessive sugar dump into your system, which can spike inflammation. The sugars found in refined carbohydrates, on the other hand, such as candies, pastries, ice cream, fruit juice and sodas, are pro-inflammatory and make muscle and nerve pain and joint inflammation worse. Sugars to avoid include cane sugar, agave syrup, maple syrup, brown rice syrup, fructose, brown sugar, turbinado sugar, sucrose, lactose, high fructose corn syrup and honey. If you need a little extra sweetness but want to avoid aggravating your pain, reach for a little monk fruit extract, stevia or coconut sugar which have zero or low glycemic affect.

Gluten

Gluten is a protein found in commonly consumed grains, such as wheat, rye, barley and some oats. It is often added in baking to bind the rest of the ingredients together and give the pastry its form and structure. But for the approximately one million people in the United States with celiac disease, accidental ingestion of gluten can cause serious health consequences, including severe abdominal pain, diarrhea or constipation, fatigue, joint pain, weight loss or weight gain. Celiac patients are missing the enzyme that allows their bodies to break down gluten, and are there intolerant of it. However, it has been estimated that up to 20 million people in the U.S. do not have celiac disease but are sensitive to gluten. Gluten intolerance and gluten sensitivity are both due to an autoimmune or allergic response that can lead to inflammatory response and pain in the body. Many of our patients have experienced substantial relief of their arthritic pain after switching to a gluten-free diet. Try avoiding gluten for a month and see if you find the reprieve others have experienced.

Cow Dairy Products

Many patients have reported over the years that when they removed cow's milk and related products from their diet, their chronic conditions like sinus problems, muscle or joint pain and eczema cleared up. When they reintroduced these items back into their diet, their conditions would relapse. The protein in cow's milk, casein, is large and often not recognizable by your immune system. Therefore your body considers it a foreign protein. People with sensitive immune systems will react adversely to foreign proteins, causing allergic reactions and in severe cases, violent inflammation and pain. Casein is also found in whey protein products. Another problem with cow's milk is lactose. Up to 70% of the world's population is lactose intolerant, which means they may suffer from bloating, gas, pain and diarrhea after consuming lactose . If you experience pain or inflammation, try skipping all productions made from cow's milk including cheese and ice cream for a month and see how you feel. Chances are, you'll notice an improvement in as little as one week.

Yeast

The typical American diet of refined carbohydrates such as pasta, breads and pastries, combined with heavy sugar intake, gives rise to dismal digestive health. Moreover, with the use of steroids, antibiotics and NSAID medications, the digestive system is further weakened by decreased gut-immunity and increased fungal or yeast organisms. This condition is called dysbiosis. For some people, the immune system's reaction to dysbiosis may be experienced as inflammation, joint or muscle pain, sinus congestion and mucus discharge, skin rash or itching. Many of our patients have benefited by cutting yeast products from their diets. To start, eliminate yeast-containing products like breads, pasta, pastries, beer, wine, cheese, milk, pickles, vinegar and products made with it, dried fruits, mushrooms, and all sugars and sweeteners. Eat only whole grains, vegetables, nuts and seeds, herbs and spices, and fish and poultry. Take high-quality probiotic supplements containing acidophilus, bifudus and other beneficial bacterial strains to help restore your gut flora and correct dysbiosis.

Fried or Grilled Food

One's of America's favorite pastimes is a good barbeque on a summer weekend. However, you might be increasing your risks for inflammation and cancer. Studies have found that frying, roasting, searing or grilling meats at high temperatures produces compounds called advanced glycation end products (AGEs), also known as glycotoxins. Browning our food helps the protein and sugar come together to form these damaging AGEs. These proteins and sugars can end up in the blood and cause it to become sticky and gummy. This interrupts the flow of our blood. High levels of AGEs in the tissues and blood can trigger an inflammatory response which induces pain and has also been linked to diabetes and cardiovascular disease.

Try reducing the cooking temperature of meats and proteins. Steam fish and seafood, simmer chicken in a sauce and braise red meat in a cooking liquid to avoid producing more AGEs.

Bad Fats

Not all fats are equal. The oil that most households and restaurants use for cooking may aggravate pain and inflammation and potentially cause other diseases. Vegetable oils such as safflower, corn, sunflower, cottonseed and canola have very high omega-6 and very low omega-3 fatty acid content. The higher omega-6 ratio promotes inflammation and may lead to pain, diabetes, heart disease and cancer. Another fat that was widely used from the 1970s until recently is trans fat. Trans fat was commonly found in fast foods and other fried products, processed snack foods, frozen breakfast products, cookies, donuts, crackers and most stick margarines. It is manufactured by hydrogenating fats, which has been discovered to trigger systemic inflammation. Avoid foods with partially hydrogenated oils in the ingredient labels. Try oils that contain high levels of omega-3 fatty acids, including extra virgin olive oil, macadamia oil, walnut oil and flax oil.

Artificial Sweeteners

Artificial sweeteners are a $25 billion industry used in many diet products. The most prevalent of the category is aspartame, which is found in more than 4,000 products worldwide. Aspartame is a neurotoxin that affects the brain and the nervous system. If you are sensitive to this chemical, your immune system will react to the foreign substance by attacking the chemical, which in return, will trigger an inflammatory response that will aggravate your pain condition. Use natural or low-glycemic sweeteners instead, such as stevia, monk fruit extract or coconut sugar.

Food Additives

Certain food additives such as monosodium glutamate (MSG), have been known to trigger inflammatory responses, including headaches, high blood pressure and weight gain. When Japanese researchers injected MSG into mice, it caused the rodents to develop significant inflammation, obesity, liver disease and type-2 diabetes. MSG is only found in processed and packaged foods as well as in restaurants, especially Japanese and Chinese restaurants. Be sure to read packaged food labels carefully, and when ordering from restaurants insist on no MSG. Ultimately your best bet is to stick with fresh, whole and unprocessed foods that are free from inflammation-inducing food additives.

Alcohol

In Chinese medicine, alcohol is recognized as a potent substance, potentially therapeutic and potentially destructive. Since ancient times, grain alcohol has been used to extract active ingredients from herbs to make medicinal tinctures. However, these tinctures were taken in minute doses and only for the duration of the treatment and discontinued after the patient's condition resolved. It has long been observed that excess alcohol can damage the liver and increase inflammation and pain. Studies show that it can also erode your intestinal lining, leading to a condition of hyper permeability of the intestinal wall called "leaky gut" syndrome. When the intestines become permeable, foreign proteins and microbes such as bacteria or yeast may enter directly into the blood stream potentially provoking immune response. Besides increasing inflammation and pain, recent studies show that there is no safe amount for alcohol consumption as it definitively increases risks of certain cancers.

Top 10 Nutritional Supplements for Healing Back Pain

Bromelain

Bromelain is the name of a group of powerful protein-digesting, or proteolytic, enzymes that are found in the pineapple plant and used as an anti-inflammatory agent after trauma or surgery. These enzymes have been widely studied and have been proven useful for reducing muscle and tissue inflammation and as a digestive aid. They help by breaking down proteins in the blood that cause inflammation, removing fibrin, the clotting material that prolongs inflammation, and reducing swelling. Bromelain is often taken as part of an inflammation-fighting formula combined with other enzymes such as papain from papaya.

Fish Oil

Fish oil contains omega-3 fatty acids, which offer significant benefits to patients suffering from inflammatory and autoimmune diseases and depression. Many of the placebo-controlled trials of fish oil in studies related to chronic inflammatory diseases revealed significant benefits, including decreased disease activity and a lowered use of anti-inflammatory drugs. The fatty acids that are specific to fish oil eicosapentaenoic acid (EPA) and docosahexaenoic acid (DHA). These are effective in decreasing the pro-inflammatory chemical interleuki 1 (IL-1), which is not only involved in arthritis but also in heart disease, multiple sclerosis and Crohn's disease. EPA and DHA also stimulate blood circulation, help to breakdown fibrin, a component of scar tissue, and can also lower blood pressure. Its use has also shown synergistic effects when paired with glucosamine. Rheumatoid arthritis patients have been shown to benefit from a daily supplement of EPA and DHA.

Type II Collagen

Cartilage is one of the primary connective tissues of the body, providing cushion and support to bones and joints. Type II collagen is the basis for articular cartilage and hyaline cartilage. It makes up 50% of all protein in cartilage and 85-90% of collagen of articular cartilage. It is the principal structural protein in cartilage that is responsible for its tensile strength and toughness. Type II collagen works with the immune system to support healthy joints and promote joint mobility and flexibility. Studies show that it's beneficial for reducing inflammation found in osteoarthritis and rheumatoid arthritis. Clinically we have found it to increase flexibility of the back and hip joints and reduce pain and swelling.

Glucosamine and Chondroitin Sulfate

Glucosamine has proven to be effective in providing long-lasting relief from arthritis-induced pain in the back and joints. In clinical studies it has been shown to rebuild cartilage, slow progression of joint degeneration and modify arthritis without side effects. Chondroitin sulfate is a protein found to decrease pain and inflammation. Occurring naturally in our cartilage, chondroitin gives the tissue its strong resistance to compression. When glucosamine and chondroitin are taken together, studies have shown them to benefit cartilage restoration, thereby reducing pain and improving joint function.

Vitamin D

Vitamin D is a fat-soluble vitamin that is naturally present in few foods except oily fish. It is also added to commercial foods and available as a dietary supplement. Vitamin D is produced in your body when you expose your skin to ultraviolet rays from sunlight. Studies have found association of severe pain with vitamin D deficiency in people with lumbar spinal stenosis. Vitamin D has other roles in the body, including modulation of cell growth, neuromuscular and immune function and reduction of inflammation. If your vitamin D levels are low, consult your healthcare provider on the appropriate dosage of supplementation.

Magnesium

Most Americans get too much calcium but not enough magnesium in their diets. Many think that a lack of calcium is why osteoporosis so prevalent, but magnesium deficiency may be the culprit. Magnesium helps with the absorption of calcium, potassium and other minerals. It also helps to curb muscle spasms in your back and fight inflammation and pain. Magnesium is also necessary for energy production within each cell in your body. It helps maintains healthy nerve and muscle function. It is also used to soften stool, calm blood pressure and alleviate anxiety. Rich natural sources of magnesium include black beans, halibut, spinach, sunflower and pumpkin seeds. Always include magnesium with calcium supplements for maximum absorption.

Boron

Boron is a trace mineral essential for healthy bones, muscles and joints. It works with calcium, magnesium and vitamin D to promote bone health. Boron also promotes sharper brain function and increases focus and memory. Studies also suggest that boron is helpful in lessening arthritis and back pain. Almonds, apricots, avocado, dates and Brazil nuts are rich in boron. It can also be taken in supplement form in trace amounts, usually combined with other vitamins in a formula.

Niacin

Niacin or vitamin B3 (nicotinic acid) is a natural anti-inflammatory that is best for your muscles, cartilage and the nerves in your back. Researchers have reported excellent results in chronic back pain and arthritis patients using niacinamide, the alkaline form of niacin which doesn't cause flushing, a common side effect with regular niacin. Other studies have shown niacin to lower cholesterol, improve memory and reverse heart disease. Niacin causes the blood vessels to dilate or open up which sometimes results in a hot, tingling sensation accompanied by a red flushing of the skin. Taking niacin immediately following a meal will lessen the flushing sensation.

MSM

Methylsulfonylmethane (MSM) has gained considerable recognition for its properties in relieving arthritis and back pain. MSM is a natural form of organic sulfur found in all living organisms, and is present in low concentrations in our body fluids and tissues. It has been found to reduce inflammation and relieve pain. It also dilates blood vessels, therefore sending a great supply of blood into your joints, and helping to relax muscle spasms. MSM is found in a variety of fresh foods, including fruits, vegetables, meat, fish and milk. However, unless your diet is composed primarily of raw foods, it is unlikely that you are receiving enough MSM for proper health management. MSM is available orally, as capsules or crystals, and can also applied topically to the skin as a lotion, cream or gel.

SAMe

SAMe, or S-adenosylmethionine, is a sulfur-containing compound. In a double-blind study comparing SAMe to the prescription anti-inflammatory drug Celebrex, the results showed no difference between the two groups; meaning that SAMe was as effective as the drug, but without the harmful side effects. SAMe seems to work as well as over-the-counter and prescription drugs for osteoarthritis, but it works more slowly. The mechanism for its anti-inflammatory property is the ability to reduce the body's production of a substance involved in cartilage destruction. It also has been found to increase cartilage production. SAMe has been widely used in Europe.

Probiotics

Pathogenic organisms can trigger immune response, causing inflammation and pain in every part of the body. Conventional approach of using antibiotic drugs to destroy bacterial pathogens often creates unanticipated consequences, such as overgrowth of pathogenic organisms that further aggravate the immune system and which can lead to chronic pain. Probiotics can counteract the negative side effects of antibiotics and supply bacteria needed for intestinal health. Lactobacillus acidophilus and lactobacillus bifidus are two types of bacteria that are found naturally and in abundance in your gastrointestinal tract—they comprise 80% of all bacterial population and are known to be health promoting. These bacteria convert sugar to lactic acid to inhibit the growth of pathogens such as E. Coli and candida albicans.

Top 10 Healing Herbs for Back Pain

White Willow Bark

Willow bark has been used in China and Europe for thousands of years, and continues to be used today for the relief of pain, headache, bursitis and tendinitis. The bark of white willow contains salicin, used to develop aspirin back in the 1800s. Salicin, in combination with the herb's powerful anti-inflammatory flavonoid compounds, produces pain-relieving and anti-inflammatory properties. Studies also show that several other components of willow bark, including polyphenols and flavonoids, have antioxidant, fever-reducing and antimicrobial properties. White willow bark is as effective as aspirin for reducing pain and inflammation.

Boswellia

Boswellia is known by several other names. It is also known as Indian Frankincense, olibanum, or Ru Xiang, in Chinese. It is the aromatic resin that is obtained from the boswellia genus of trees. The name "frankincense" derives from its introduction to Europe by Frankish crusaders. Originally from the Middle East, boswellia has historically been used in religious rites described in the Old Testament. In Chinese medicine, it has been used for arthritic inflammation, back pain relief and to improve circulation.

Corydalis

Corydalis root, or Yan Hu Suo, is part of the fume wort family, and related to the poppy family. It is traditionally used to activate blood flow, remove stagnant blood and relieve pain. Often used as a safe and natural analgesic and calming agent in Chinese medicine, corydalis has been found to possess compounds similar to those found in Western anti-inflammatory, analgesic and allergy medications, and has also been known to improve heart function and aid in restful sleep. Corydalis can be taken in tea or capsule form by itself for pain relief, but it is often used as part of a formula with other herbs, such as the Arthritis/Joint formula.

Siberian Ginseng

Eleuthero root, or Ci Wu Jia, is also commonly known as Siberian ginseng. Traditionally known as a tonic for aging and related symptoms, notably lower back pain and joint weakness, it is also famously used as an herbal tonic liqueur. Research in Russia and Korea has yielded troves of information on the herb. It has been found to be an adaptogen, helpful in assisting the body to combat stress and recover from adrenal fatigue. Additionally, eleuthero has been found to contain compounds that function as antioxidants and anti-inflammatories, and that help to lower cholesterol and enhance immune system repair. It may also prove helpful in increasing endurance, and improving learning and memory functions. It can be taken in tea or capsule form, but is often used as part of a formula with other herbs, such as the DuraBone formula.

Dipsacus

The name for dipsacus root in Chinese, Xu Duan, translates to "restore what is broken." Indeed, this herb's primary function is to assist in healing traumatic injuries, especially to the lower parts of your body. According to Chinese medicine, dipsacus root strengthens bones and connective tissue like tendons and ligaments. To this point, it treats conditions like weak, sore, stiff and painful lower back and knees, as well as osteopenia and osteoporosis. In addition to strengthening the body, dipsacus root can also strengthen the mind by helping to treat memory loss. It can be taken in tea or capsule form, but is often used as part of a formula with other herbs, such as the DuraBone formula.

Myrrh

Myrrh is the dried sap or resin of the Commiphora myrrha tree, and is native to Eastern Africa and the southern region of the Middle East. It is a bitter substance that, along with its medicinal properties, is used in incense, perfumes and as an additive to wine. It enjoyed cultural prominence in ancient Greek and Roman civilizations. Myrrh has similar uses to that of frankincense, though according to traditional Chinese medicine, myrrh moves blood while frankincense moves energy. Similarly, in Ayurvedic medicine, myrrh is used for circulatory problems. Traditionally, Myrrh is used for toothache pain, arthritis, tendonitis, sciatica, rheumatism, herpes, asthma, cough, bronchial conditions, cold hands and feet and gum disease. It is also used to balance the immune system. It can be taken in tea or capsule form, but is often used as part of a formula with other herbs, such as the Arthritis/Joint formula and the DuraBone formula.

Valerian Root

Valerian root is a perennial flowering plant that is native to Europe and Asia. It has a history of being an ancient remedy for insomnia, and it is also known for its relaxant and anti-spasm properties. Known as "nature's tranquilizer," valerian root was used as a sleep sedative in the United States until after World War II, when it was replaced by synthetic drug alternatives. Valerian root is used to regulate the nervous system and relieve sleeplessness without creating a sense of grogginess in the user the following morning. Traditionally, valerian has been used to treat anxiety, nervousness, irritability, nervous exhaustion and stress, muscle pain and spasm, irritable bowel syndrome and hypertension.

Achryanthes

Achryanthes or "ox knee" as it is called in Chinese medicine, is used to improve circulation in the lower half of the body. It is beneficial to joints and bones and used for pain and soreness of the lower back and knees. Due to its function of increasing blood circulation it is also been used traditionally for high blood pressure, painful menstruation and amenorrhea. It has the ability to clear painful urination accompanied with blood in the urine. Achryanthes lowers blood cholesterol levels and is used in the treatment of atherosclerosis. The root juice is used in Nepal for toothache.

Cinnamon

Cinnamon has been a staple of Chinese herbal medicine for thousands of years. It comes from the cassia tree, an evergreen native to Southeast Asia. Cinnamon has a myriad of uses in herbal medicine. Generally, it is used as a warming agent, treating all sorts of cold issues, from the common cold to arthritic or muscle pain that is worsened by cold weather. Cinnamon is also an energizing herb used to treat fatigue and low energy. The following are just a few of the conditions that cinnamon is traditionally used to treat: arterial plaque, arthritis, carpal tunnel syndrome (CTS), cold hands and feet, cold, flu, lumbar pain, muscle injury, sciatica, tendonitis, as well as varicose and spider veins. Recent research suggests that cinnamon taken orally can aid insulin's effectiveness, which is quite significant for diabetics.

Peach Kernel

Peach kernels have been used as part of Chinese herbal therapy for thousands of years. After a ripe peach is picked, the stone is taken out and broken to get the kernel, which is then dried in the sunlight. The kernel is broken up before using, though it should not be broken into small pieces until it is to be used to prevent oxidation of the therapeutic essential oils. Peach kernel is traditionally used for traumatic injury with bruising and pain, menstrual pain and disorders, abdominal pain and abdominal masses. It is often combined with safflower in herbal formulations. Peach kernel is rich in oils that lubricate and relax the bowels, and for this reason it is also used to treat constipation due to dryness in the intestines.

Chapter Five

Bridging Mind and Body: Breathing and Meditation to Relax Your Back

Ancient medical traditions, including Chinese medicine, have long observed that psychological and emotional factors can and often do cause physical changes that can aggravate or sometimes even cause back pain. It was explained five thousand years ago in the Yellow Emperor's Classic of Medicine that when the spirit is disturbed, it creates chaos in the qi—leading to blockages that can lead to pain and dysfunction. To achieve resolution of the condition one must calm the spirit and unblock qi stagnation, thereby relieving the source of pain and tension.

In modern times, Dr. John Sarno, physician and professor of physical medicine at New York University, defined the theory of Tension Myositis Syndrome (TMS). According Dr. Sarno, emotional tension is pushed out of awareness and enters the unconscious. Unconscious tension causes changes in the body's nervous system. Constriction of blood vessels and reduction of blood flow affect soft tissue in the back: muscles, tendons, ligaments and nerves. This constriction results in decrease in oxygen, buildup of biochemical waste products in the muscles, muscle tension, muscle spasm and back pain.

TMS is significant because if one's back pain is primarily caused by psychological and emotional stress, resuming a full range of physical activity and exercise is actually beneficial. Treatment for stress-induced back pain is multi-disciplinary, incorporating physical, emotional, cognitive and environmental factors. Techniques such as acupuncture (see chapter three), meditation, creative visualization, journaling, cognitive behavioral therapy, and mind-body practices like qi gong (see chapter six) can help release stress and stop the vicious circle of stress-induced back pain.

Meditation Is as Ancient as Chinese Medicine

For more than 5,000 years, Chinese medicine has refined the use of meditation to build the body's life force, facilitate healing, reduce stress and relieve pain. And modern scientists agree. The well-documented effects of regular meditation include lowered blood pressure, less heart disease, decreased chronic pain and increased mental clarity. Meditation is an indispensable tool for living a longer, richer life and avoiding the burnout that comes from constant stress.

Beginning Meditation

Many people find the idea of meditation to be daunting. They think they do not have the time, saying, "Someday I will devote the time to study meditation." Meditation is simple. You don't need much training and you don't need to be alone in the mountains. You can learn it right now! All you need is a quiet place to sit and the curiosity to try it. Practice meditation in a quiet environment. Begin with 10 to 15 minutes. The morning is the best time, but anytime you can find an uninterrupted and quiet chunk of time will work. One warning: never meditate after eating. Silence your phone and close the door to any other possible interruptions.

Make it Easier, Try Chair Meditation

Sit comfortably in a chair with your spine erect and both legs and thighs forming a ninety-degree angle with the ground, keeping your feet at shoulder width apart. Start by breathing as naturally as possible. After a few times, try breathing with your abdomen only. Slowly, your breath will deepen as you practice. You notice that babies breathe with their abdomen, but as we grow older, we become affected by our stress, lifestyle and environment and begin to breathe from the chest. For meditation, breathe deep and low from the abdomen.

Sitting Meditation in a Half Lotus

One basic method for sitting meditation is to sit on a cushion on the floor in half lotus position, with the dorsal side of your left foot resting on the right inner thigh or on the forward third of a chair. The spine is straight and vertical as if piercing the sky. The back of the left hand rests on the palm of the right hand with the tips of thumbs lightly touching. The back of the right hand either rests on the left heel, if sitting on the floor, or on the lap if sitting on a chair. Elbows remain slightly bent and separated from the ribs. The trapezius and shoulders are relaxed. The mouth is closed with the tip of the tongue lightly touching the upper palate. Eyelids are relaxed and remain slightly opened and unfocused. Ear lobes, trapezius and shoulders are aligned in one horizontal line. Set the posture by gently swinging right and left, front and back and then stop at the center to begin meditation.

Let Your Mind Run its Course

Begin to quiet your mind. Of course, the thoughts will come—and they will always be there. Don't struggle against them. Let the thoughts come, but don't dwell on them. Keep relaxing, and bring your consciousness back to your breath. If you have trouble concentrating, focus on a word or a mantra that invokes a calming effect within you. In meditation, you need not think anything. You need not feel anything in particular. Sitting meditation is not thought, but action...just keep the spine straight. If your mind clings to thoughts, you can count exhalations until you don't need to anymore. The brain is a sensory organ that does not turn off even when we sleep. So don't expect to turn it off during meditation. As long as you do not attach to any thought and as long as you stay present, you will be meditating authentically.

Meditation Reduces Stress and Relieves Pain

Meditation has been shown to provide benefits to the back pain sufferer. It is known to reduce stress and relieve pain. Contrary to common misconception, meditation is not an intellectual practice but a practice of action. It provides an opportunity to spend some time each day to be in the present—observing, listening, smelling and feeling the current moment. It provides an opportunity to let go, for mental peace and stillness. It's time to detach oneself from the incessant mental chatter that distorts our view of the world, preventing us from seeing things whole. Furthermore, the act of keeping the spine straight during meditation strengthens the back.

Don't worry or be critical of whether you are meditating correctly. Just know that if you feel quiet and relaxed and you are paying attention to your breathing, you are on the right path. With continued practiced, your body will know how to relax more quickly and the healing and wisdom of deep practice will come to you.

Stress Release Meditation

Stress, often called "the silent killer," is the root of many illnesses: from high blood pressure and heart disease to cancer and depression. You can learn how to release the stress and tension build-up through this simple stress release meditation.

Sit comfortably or lie down on your back. Slow your respiration to deep, abdominal breathing. Utter the word "calm" in your mind with every exhalation. You will be visualizing the relaxation of a body part and releasing tension with every exhalation. Trace the following three pathways outlined below.

Guided Meditation for Stress Release

Start on top of your head. Inhale and then exhale while visualizing your scalp muscles relaxing. Say "calm" in your mind. Repeat this with each body part as you move down through your face, throat, chest, stomach, abdomen, thighs, knees, legs, ankles and feet. When you've relaxed your feet, visualize all the tension in your body leaving through your toes as dark smoke.

Start from the temples of your head. This path focuses on the sides and upper extremities. Inhale and then exhale while visualizing your temple muscles relaxing. Say the word "calm" in your mind. Repeat this with each body part as you move down through your jaws, the sides of your neck, shoulders, upper arms, elbows, forearms, wrists and hands. Once you've relaxed your hands, visualize all the tension leaving your body via your fingertips as dark smoke.

The final pathway begins on the back of your head. This path relaxes the back side of your body. Repeat the breathing-visualization-word routine as you go from the back of your neck to your upper back, middle back, lower back, back of thighs, calves and heels.

Repeat this sequence until you feel free from tension. Practice this for 15 minutes every day. If you feel that you would be more successful with a guide, try our Meditation for Stress Release audio CD (available at wellnesslivingstore.com or download from iTunes by Dr. Maoshing Ni)

Pain-Tamer Visualization

Visualization meditation is one of the most powerful pain management tools, used with great effectiveness by pain specialists, psychologists and biofeedback therapists. Learn to erase your pain with this meditation.

Sit or lie quietly, and breathe slowly. With each exhale, feel your tension subside until you are completely relaxed. Visualize fine vertical lines running through your body from head to toe. Keep breathing deeply as you tune in to these lines. Now bring your focus to the painful area of your body and visualize crisscross lines at the spot that hurts. Using your imagination, erase the crisscross lines that intersect and disrupt the smooth vertical ones. Slowly, one line at a time, erase the cross-hatching with your mind until only the verticals are left. You've created a mental picture of your body's energy meridians and restored their smooth flow. You may also try my Pain Management Meditation CD to help guide you (available at wellnesslivingstore.com).

Five Clouds Meditation for Energizing

This is a simple meditation practice that can help you energize your internal organs. In traditional Chinese medicine, there are five organ systems in the body along with five elements. Five Clouds meditation involves visualizing the elemental colors associated with each of the five organ systems. The five colors corresponding to the five organ systems are green for the liver, red for the heart, yellow for the spleen, white for the lungs, and blue for the kidneys. Start by imagining a gathering cloud of the corresponding color enveloping the organ, in the order given. Take two to five minutes for each organ system. When you have completed all five clouds, expand them so that the five colors intermix, ultimately becoming a rainbow. You may want to try following a guided audio CD Five Clouds Meditation (available at wellnesslivingstore.com).

Correct Breath, Correct Mind

Once the meditation form is in place, we can bring our attention to the breath. The key is not to force it and to simply allow breathing. Allow the breath to travel through the area below the navel. Inhale with a relaxed diaphragm and allow the breath to fill every space within the lungs. Exhale slowly from the lower abdomen. After the breath is completely expelled, the body will breathe in naturally to begin another breath cycle. After you correct your breathing, only then can you correct your mind.

The Power of Journaling

If you don't have a bowel movement for several days, you're not only constipated, you're filled with wastes and toxins that can damage your health. The same thing happens with your mind. Negative thoughts, feelings and images can linger and become "toxic," affecting your thought patterns and behaviors subconsciously. To quell this "mental constipation," write in a journal at the end of the day to unload all the negativity you have experienced. Writing it out allows you to reflect, understand a situation and observe your feelings. For the ultimate elimination, rip out the journal pages and burn them. You will feel clearer and lighter in your being.

Expect Better Outcomes With CBT

The brain is a neutral object that will respond in the way you train it to respond. Cognitive Behavioral Therapy (CBT) trains it to be rational. Because of your history, you may expect things to turn out poorly and become anxious or depressed, which in turn causes physiological changes that affect your back pain. With CBT you learn to question whether your old beliefs are rational or not. Are they based on fact? What is the real truth? Have you considered there may be no legitimate reason to feel anxious and fearful? As thoughts change your beliefs, then physical changes occur in the brain, which has been demonstrated by using brain imaging technology. You learn with CBT to expect different outcomes, because you now believe differently than you did in the past. When you expect better outcomes, better outcomes occur and you are able to more effectively manage your fears, anxiety and negativity.

Chapter Six

Moving with Grace and Strength: Exercise and "Qi Gong" for a Strong Back

This program to strengthen the back integrates cardio exercise with rehabilitative qi gong, long a part of Chinese medicine. Most back pain conditions can be resolved and prevented through non-surgical means. Treatment modalities such as acupuncture, tuina bodywork, herbal and nutritional therapies, physical therapy and medications, and injection are all non-invasive rehabilitation methods to resolve pain. However, for sustained relief from back pain you need to take an active role in strengthening your own back. Exercise is the healing modality that happens to be one of the most effective in preventing and resolving back injury.

A consistent and appropriate regimen of exercise is extremely effective in activating the muscles that support the back. In activating these muscles, you restore and enhance the functionality of the musculature. Consequently, the supporting muscles become stronger and capable in relieving the pressure on the spinal joints, allowing these joints to move more freely with less restriction. As you reduce the strain on the spinal joints, your joints become less vulnerable to injury.

Exercise Is Better for Your Bones Than Milk

You don't have to drink a gallon of milk to have strong bones. When you exercise, you bear more weight on the bones, and this weight-bearing activity helps to prevent or delay osteoporosis, a condition in which bones lose their density and become more prone to fracture. Exercise also allows muscles to stretch and contract, increasing circulation of blood and nutrients. Blood circulation is also essential in the removal of wastes, such as lactic acid, that may remain stagnant in the back and become an irritant to the nerves.

Exercise Relieves Stress so You Can Sleep Like a Baby

Stress aggravates pain. By reducing stress through exercise, we are more likely to reduce pain. Exercise relieves stress by triggering the release of endorphins, the body's own natural pain relievers. It also helps to promote healthy sleep, as the increase in endorphins also increases serotonin, a neurochemical that regulates mood and sleep. And good sleep helps to optimize your self-healing potential, immune system and quality of life. It's a virtuous cycle—exercise relieves stress which lowers pain and helps sleep, and good sleep in turn improves healing

Personalization Is Key to Success

There is one thing to keep in mind before beginning an exercise program to strengthen the back. The exercise MUST be appropriate for the individual and MUST be executed with the correct form. If these two conditions are not met when embarking on an exercise program, the exercise may actually aggravate the pain and worsen injury of the back. Do not do any exercise that causes pain. If the back pain worsens after exercise, you must decrease and modify your activity. Make sure to consult with qualified health care professionals before beginning any exercise program. This is especially important if you have had surgery, osteoporosis, arthritis or any acute or chronic injury of the spine. This is also important if you are pregnant.

(Check out Qi Gong for Prenatal Health at wellnesslivingstore.com.)

Scheduling Time to Exercise

Select a time and place in which you are able to complete an exercise session consisting of warm up, primary exercises and cool down with minimal distraction. If possible, complete your exercise session around the same time each day so that it becomes a part of your daily routine. A 10-minute exercise session every other day is better than a 30-minute exercise session once a week or once a month. Feel free to integrate quick and easy exercises into your daily life. For example, you can subtly mobilize and stretch your neck, thoracic spine and lumbar spine at your desk or on your couch in between working, reading or watching television and take stairs instead of elevators wherever you go.

Comfort and Safety Are Fundamental to Exercise

Make sure you dress appropriately for your exercise session. Loose, comfortable clothing is best. Do not exercise immediately after eating or when you're tired. Do not exercise when you need to urinate or have a bowel movement. To reduce the chance of injury or accident, make sure that the surface that you are exercising on is not slippery. Using an exercise mat is recommended. And make sure you have enough space to move. By ensuring comfort and safety you maximize the benefits of exercise and lower the risk of aggravating your pain condition.

Mindful Breathing and Moving

Pay attention to your breath and be mindful of your bodily movements. Deep breathing brings nutrients and oxygen to working muscles and optimizes the beneficial effects of exercise. Likewise, pay attention to the contraction and extension of your muscles. How is your form? How do you feel? Do not overdo it, for overexertion increases the risk for injury. Synchronize your breath with each movement. Take short breaks between sets to reset the body, avoiding stiffness and fatigue. Visualizing the flow of the qi energy throughout the body is also helpful in generating strength, making the exercise more enjoyable and comfortable.

A comprehensive exercise routine for a healthy back is comprised of Warm Up, Primary Exercises and Cool Down.

Warm Up and Cool Down When You Exercise

Many of our patients injure themselves engaging in even gentle disciplines like yoga and pilates, because they don't take the time to properly warm up before exercise and cool down afterward. Our muscles get cold and stiff from even brief stints of sitting or lying down. We advise gentle stretching and warming your body with proper clothing or heat packs before you begin. Many gyms and health clubs have saunas, an excellent way to warm up before an exercise session. Afterward, cool the muscles with a shower or use a cold pack, especially on areas where you feel muscle or joint pain.

Get Your Heart and Body Moving

Cardio exercise comes in all forms. Brisk walking, jogging, biking, dancing, the elliptical machine, jump rope, martial arts and even tai chi can be good for your cardiovascular system as long as you are able to get your heart rate to sustain above 120 beats per minute for at least 20 minutes. You should do cardio exercise at least 4-5 times a week and strive for 30 to 45 minutes during each session.

Warm Up with Foundation Exercises
For Tai Chi and Qi Gong

When beginning any tai chi or qi gong practice, it is traditional to start by practicing the foundation exercises. These are used to loosen and open up the various joints of the body, allowing blood, qi and body fluids to pass through the joints with ease. These exercises are also very useful when beginning any other types of exercise. When practiced regularly, you will experience more graceful movements, minimized joint strain and increased strength and energy. Moreover, physical and emotional stressors are released during the short routines outlined in the following pages. Start by tapping the trunk, arms and legs to activate energy and awaken lymphatic circulation. Move on to loosening the joints by circling each joint of the body, then finally bouncing and shaking the body for bone and muscle strengthening. These exercises should be performed with ease and can easily be modified to accommodate weak or painful joints.

Tapping the Trunk to Awaken Energy

Place your feet shoulder-width apart with your arms hanging loose at your sides. Shift your weight back and forth from one foot to the other, while turning the pelvis at the same time. The weight should be mostly on the left leg while turning the pelvis to the left, and then shifted to the opposite leg as your position changes. This should create enough momentum for your arms to swing in front and behind you. With loose fists, allow them to alternately tap the lower abdomen below the navel and at a similar height on the back. Repeat this movement several times. Continue this turning and tapping while raising the position of where your fists land, moving from the lower abdomen up to the shoulders, tracing a "V" formation, and mirroring this tapping by moving your fists up your back as well. Then tap back down the same path, ending on the lower abdomen and back once again.

Tapping the Arms

With your feet shoulder-width apart, extend your left arm forward at shoulder height. Making a loose fist with your right hand, lightly tap your trunk, starting just beneath the navel, moving along your left side and upward to underneath your left armpit. Move the tapping up your left shoulder to the neck, back down your shoulder and down the inside of your left arm to the palm. Tap up the outside of your left arm, up to the shoulder and neck. When finished, gently shake out your left arm. Repeat this sequence on your right side while tapping with your left fist.

Tapping the Back and Legs

Start by rubbing your palms a few times in a circular motion over your lower back and kidney area. The circle should move up the spine, then downwards alongside the spine. With loose fists, tap (using the inner side of your fist with your thumb and first finger) over your lower back in a similar circular pattern several times. Next, place your feet wide apart with your legs straight. Bend at the waist, and using the palm side of your fists, tap down the outer aspect of the buttocks, thighs, legs and ankles. Tap up the inner ankles, legs and thighs, straightening your body as you go. Bring your feet back to shoulder-width apart. Tap the area that connects the thighs to the pelvis several times and, with each tap, alternate between slightly bent and straightened knees.

Swing the Arms and Jump for Cardio Stimulation

Place your feet shoulder-width apart. Gently swing your arms downward in front of your body and behind to the back, letting the swing take your arms upward. Reverse the swing from the back to the front. Repeat this several times, inhaling as your arms move backward and exhaling as they come forward. Allow a natural resistance to inform how far to swing in either direction. Enhance the swing by bending your knees as your arms swing down past the front of your body, and as your arms reach up in the back, lift your heels. After several more swings, jump up as your arms move back and up. You should feel the backward/upward movement of your arms naturally carries you into a jump at the end of the swing. Jump several times, going higher with each swing. Then progressively jump lower until you stop jumping, slowing the back and forth of the arm swing until you're standing still. This practice has been shown to improve cardiovascular capacity.

Joint Rotations to Open and Restore Joints

Once vital energy, blood circulation and the lymphatic system are awakened and activated by tapping your trunk and extremities, you need to be sure that the flow isn't obstructed at the joints. Within the foundation practices are movements that circle the joints and open up the flow of synovial fluids to nourish and restore joint functions. These joint rotations should be done gently and slowly, without any strain whatsoever. With consistent practice you will naturally experience an increase in the range of motion in your joints.

Neck Rotation

Place your heels together and face your feet forward. Place your left hand on the lower abdomen, with the right hand on top of the left. Allowing gravity to do the work in moving your head, gently tilt your torso to the left side, allowing your head to lean to the left, then the back, right and front. Repeat three times in each direction, inhaling as the head goes back and exhaling as it comes forward again. This is a whole body movement, allowing your head to follow the gravitational pull.

Shoulder Rotation

Lift your left shoulder and roll it backward, down, forward and up, making sure to keep your arms relaxed. Repeat three times in each direction. Repeat on your right shoulder. Inhale while circling up and exhale while circling down.

Breathe from the bottom up. Relax, close your eyes for three minutes and breathe. Like a baby, breathe from low in your abdomen, filling up your lungs from the bottom. Many people breathe primarily from the chest and shoulders, which only worsens feelings of tightness in the upper section of the torso. Breathing from the bottom up will gradually undo this pattern of breathing, and can also help to relieve tension and support a more natural posture. Practice this way of breathing twice daily for two weeks.

A quick tension release can be performed by exaggerating the tension before relaxing the muscles. On an inhale, pull your shoulders up high, as close to the ears as possible. Be careful not to overdo it, and stop if you feel any pain. Stretch just enough to feel a moderate pressure. You can emphasize the muscle contraction by squeezing your eyes shut on the same inhale. As you exhale, drop your shoulders, breathe out through an open mouth and open and relax your eyes. Sense the difference in your neck and shoulders. You can repeat this several times daily.

Wrist Rotation

Clasp your hands together with your fingers interlaced. Leading with the thumbs, trace a horizontal figure eight in front of your body with your hands, making sure to maximize the range of motion with your wrists. You can start with a small figure eight, gradually making it larger with each revolution, before reversing the motion to lead with the pinkies, and making the figure eight movements smaller once again. Breathe naturally and deep.

Hip and Waist Rotation

Start with your feet wide apart (double the width of your shoulders) and legs straight. Place your hands on the sides of your waist. Bend forward at the waist. Keeping your hands in place, turn from the waist and bring your upper body to the left, circling up to standing with a slight back bend, down on the right side, before bending forward again. Repeat three times in both directions. Inhale when circling to the back, exhale when circling to the front.

Knee Rotation

With your feet together, bend at the waist to rest your hands on your knees. Gently rub them to warm them up. Keeping your palms centered on the upper ridge of the kneecaps, bend your knees to make a circle, pushing toward your left side, then circling them around in front to the right, then straightening back up. Repeat three times in both directions. Next, keeping your knees together, bend them forward and then separate to each side, circling back to center as you straighten your legs. Repeat three times. Reverse the direction of the circles and repeat three more times. Exhale when your knees bend down, inhale when straightening the legs.

Ankle Rotation

Lift your left foot and rotate it at the ankle three times in both directions. Point and flex the foot, then shake the ankle and the entire leg to loosen the joints. Repeat on your other foot. Your breathing should be deep and natural.

Bouncing Your Center

With your feet shoulder-width apart, your spine straight and arms hanging loosely by your sides, gently bounce your whole body, focusing your center of gravity around the pelvis area. The bouncing should start at the balls of your feet and all the joints should be involved in the motion. While most of the movement will come from bending your knees, this motion should elicit a gentle vibration to move the energy to all parts of your body. Sometimes you will bounce vigorously and other times more gently. Follow what your body needs in the moment. This bouncing movement can be performed on its own for a few seconds or up to several minutes at a time when a simple body-wide stimulation—and relaxation—is desired. When completed, take a moment to feel the sensations moving through your body. Vibrating the body in this way has been shown to promote bone strength. And when bones are strong, the tissues and joints attached to them are strong as well.

Achieve Optimum Health with Qi Gong

Qi gong is a branch of traditional Chinese medicine that aligns breath, body and intention. It was originated and developed by individuals of ancient times who observed the connection between people and nature. The cultivation practices that they developed based on these observations turned out to be extremely effective in achieving optimum health. They also happen to be great for the back.

In qi gong, qi refers to vital energy and gong refers to cultivation, work, practice, mastery and skill. Only in the recent decades has qi gong been introduced and become accessible in western society. In the traditional context, qi is simply the ubiquitous force of the universe. All living beings are believed to channel this universal energy and express it as vitality and power. How well a living being expresses qi or vitality depends on how healthy this living being is. Qi gong is a means of cultivating your most fundamental aspect of health, your vital energy.

Restore Your Healthy Bioelectric Energy

In the modern context, qi is most closely associated with electromagnetic energy. And more specifically, in the context of the human body, qi refers to the electromagnetic energy of human tissue known as bioelectricity. Human tissue is alive and electrically conducive, and therefore forms an electromagnetic field and circuit. If the body is an electromagnetic field, then this field of energy is affected by infinite variables, including our environment, actions, thoughts, emotions and the food and fluid we consume. Biochemical reactions through the assimilation of food and air generate qi that is circulated by electromotive forces within the body. Therefore, an injury of the back is an injury of not only muscles, tendons, ligaments and bones, but also an injury of your bioelectrical field.

Qi Gong for Healthy Back

Qi gong focuses on balancing qi or bioelectric energy and is best learned through the instructional DVD: Qi Gong for a Healthy Back (available at wellnesslivingstore.com) or through a qualified instructor (chihealth. org). The following is a series of specific qi gong practices to help restore health to your back and relieve pain. We suggest that you start with Beginning Practice and after a few weeks of working with the movements and as you feel your back getting stronger and less pain to then graduate to Intermediate and finally Advance Practice. Progress at your own pace and stop if you experience increased pain. Go back to doing what makes you feel good. We suggest that you do these exercises on a daily basis, if possible. The more you practice, the stronger your back and core will become, thus improving your chance of keeping back pain away. If you are suffering from a back injury, consult with your health care practitioners before engaging in any exercise.

Beginner Practice

Lying Down Practice
(Upon waking and before bedtime)

1. Awaken from Sleep
As your neck comes up to gaze at your toes, which are now flexed toward your head, reach down with your hands to the side of your legs. Hold this position for a few seconds and repeat three times.

2. Stretch Ankles and Straighten Legs
Bring your left knee to your chest and grasp with both hands. Rotate your ankle three times one way and three times the other way. Straighten your leg with the sole of your foot, slowly returning your leg back to starting position. Repeat three times on both sides.

3. Stretching Knees Like A Butterfly Opening Wings
Bring your knee to your chest, and grasp with both hands. Simultaneously bring your chin to your knee. Straighten your leg with the sole of your foot toward the ceiling and slowly return to starting position. Repeat three times on both sides.

Bring both legs to your chest and grasp with both hands. Bring your chin to your chest and release. Raise the soles of your feet to the ceiling and lower your legs back to starting position. Repeat three times.

4. Stretch like a Cat
Kneel on your legs with your feet tucked under your hips and buttocks. Bring your chin to the floor with your arms outstretched in front of you. Transition forward to a cat stance with your hands underneath your shoulders and your back upwards to the sky, while tucking your pelvis underneath and your chin into your chest. Transition back to starting position and repeat a total of three times.

5. Massage Kidneys in Circles

Sitting on your knees with feet under your hips, massage your kidney area at the lower lumbar area. Repeat for about 50 circles.

Standing Practice

6. Weeping Willow Sways in the Morning Breeze

Stand with your feet hips-width apart, pelvis tucked slightly under, chin back with your eyes pointing forward. Bring feet together. Cup hands in front of your navel area. Slowly rotate your head and neck three times one way and repeat in the opposite direction. Bring feet hips-width apart and place hands with palms behind your lower lumbar. Rotate your hips in a circle three times one way and repeat on the opposite direction. Bring feet together. Place both hands on your knees. Rotate both knees together one direction and repeat in the opposite direction. Then separate your knees apart from each other in a circular motion, with hands still on your knees.

7. Jade Plate Receives Morning Dew

With heels together and toes pointed 45 degrees outward, touch your right thumb and forefingers together and place at your lower lumbar spine with fingers pointing upwards. With your left hand, move your arm across your belt line, palm side up, and make a circle going away from your body toward your left side, with hand finishing palm up by the left ear. Push your palm to the sky while pushing down with your right hand towards the floor. Do this movement three times and repeat on the opposite side.

8. Flying Crane Gracefully Lands

With feet slightly wider than shoulder width, begin squatting while placing your palms on your lumbar/kidney area. While rising, with a faster motion, sweep your hands upward to end in front of your body at eye level, palm side down. Squat while slowly lowering your hands to the top of your knees. Repeat the kidney sweeping motion upward while rising, and return to the squat position with hands on knees. Repeat once more for a total of three times.

Chair Sitting Practice

9. Solid as a Mountain

Sit toward the front of the chair, with knees bent around 90 degrees, pelvis tucked under and chin inwards with head erect. Sit for one minute, breathing through your abdomen.

10. Huddle Your Thighs

Bend forward to touch hands to the floor, head hanging between your knees. Breathe slowly through your abdomen. Return to starting position.

11. Gathering Your Energy

From standing position, gather the energy upward towards the top of your head and draw down the front side of your body. Gather again and hold your hands in front of your eyes.

Lower arms down to the chest position and hold. Next, lower arms down to the lower Dan Tien, below the belly button, position and hold. Finally, relax hands to original start position.

Daily practice of qi gong is key to a healthy back, and possessing a strong back is the foundation to an active and fulfilling life. For further assistance, refer to the instructional DVD: Qi Gong for a Healthy Back, available at wellnesslivingstore.com

Intermediate Practice

Lying Down Practice
(Upon waking and before bedtime)

1. Awaken from Sleep
As your neck comes up to gaze at your toes, which are now flexed toward your head, reach down with your hands to the side of your legs. Hold this position for a few seconds and repeat three times.

2. Stretch Ankles and Straighten Legs
Bring your left knee to your chest and grasp with both hands. Rotate your ankle three times one way and three times the other way. Straighten your leg with the sole of your foot toward the ceiling and slowly return your leg back to starting position. Repeat three times on both sides.

3. Stretching Knees Like A Butterfly Opening Wings
Bring your knee to your chest, and grasp with both hands. While doing this movement bring your chin to your knee. Straighten your leg with the sole of your foot toward the ceiling and slowly return to starting position. Repeat three times on both sides.

Bring both legs to your chest and grasp with both hands. Bring your chin to your chest and release. Raise the soles of your feet to the ceiling and lower your legs back to starting position. Repeat three times.

4. Stretch Like a Cat
Kneel on your legs with your feet tucked under your hips and buttocks. Bring your chin to the floor with your arms outstretched in front of you. Transition forward to a cat stance with your hands underneath your shoulders and your back upwards to the sky, while tucking your pelvis underneath and your chin into your chest. Transition back to starting position and repeat for a total of three times.

5. Massage Kidneys in Circles

Sitting on your knees with your feet under your hips, massage your kidney area at the lower lumbar area. Repeat for about 50 circles.

6. Raise Legs and Ride a Bicycle

From a lying position, raise both legs toward your chest. Pedal like you would riding a bicycle, extending your alternating legs toward the floor and back again.

7. Wriggle Like a Young Dragon

From a sitting position, extend one leg with the opposite leg planted on the floor close to you. Your hands will be on the floor behind you, palm side down. Push with your planted foot while extending your hip to the ceiling, creating a table-like position. Head stays in a neutral position, with eyes looking toward the ceiling at the apex of the move. Repeat three times on each side.

Standing Practice

8. Weeping Willow Sways in the Morning Breeze

Stand with your feet hips-width apart, pelvis tucked slightly under, chin back with your eyes pointing forward. Bring feet together. Cup hands in front of your navel area. Slowly rotate your head and neck three times one way and repeat in the opposite direction. Bring feet hips-width apart and place hands with palms behind your lower lumbar. Rotate your hips in a circle three times one way and repeat on the opposite direction. Next, bring your feet together. Place both hands on your knees. Rotate both knees together one direction and repeat in the opposite direction. Then separate your knees apart from each other in a circular motion, with hands still on your knees.

9. Jade Plate Receives Morning Dew

With heels together and toes pointed 45 degrees outward, touch your right thumb and forefingers together and place at your lower lumbar spine with fingers pointing upwards. With your left hand, move your arm across your belt line, palm side up, and make a circle going away from your body toward your left side, with hand finishing palm up by the left ear. Push your palm to the sky while pushing down with your right hand towards the floor. Do this movement three times and repeat on the opposite side.

10. Flying Crane Gracefully Lands

With feet slightly wider than shoulder width, begin squatting while placing your palms on your lumbar/kidney area. While rising, with a faster motion, sweep your hands upward to end in front of your body at eye level, palm side down. Squat while slowly lowering your hands to the top of your knees. Repeat the kidney sweeping motion upward while rising, and return to the squat position with hands on knees. Repeat once more for a total of three times.

11. Pushing the Mountain

Begin with your feet close together. Use both arms to make three wide circles, starting from your hip, to your shoulders, over your head, and complete the circle in a sweeping motion. At the end of the third repetition, take a large step out to the side and while transferring weight to the extended leg, push your arms like you are holding a giant boulder overhead, stretching the sides of your body over the extended leg. Shift your weight back and repeat, pushing the mountain three times. At the end of the last push, begin three circles in the opposite position while returning to the original starting stance. Step out to the side again and push the mountain to the opposite side three more times. Return to starting position.

12. Beauty Admires Herself in the Pond

With your feet shoulder-width apart, make clockwise circles with your arms from your waist to over your head three times. Toward the top of the third repetition, your right hand stays under your left arm, with your hand flexed away from you. Your left extends behind your head, with your elbow pointing skyward, and your hand flexed away from your midline. Look toward your right foot and push both arms on opposite directions. Do this three times. Repeat on the opposite side, beginning with circles in a counterclockwise direction. Place your right hand behind your head, your left hand under your arms and press in opposite directions three times.

Chair Sitting Practice

13. Solid as a Mountain

Sit toward the front of the chair, with knees bent around 90 degrees, pelvis tucked under and chin inwards with head erect. Sit for one minute, breathing through your abdomen.

14. Huddle Your Thighs

Bend forward to touch hands to the floor, head hanging between your knees. Breathe slowly through your abdomen. Return to starting position.

15. Arms Stretch Above and to the Sides.

While sitting, clasp hands in front of your chest and extend them overhead. Next, draw your hands down to chin level, and extend arms upward to the left, and then again to the right. Finish by extending arms overhead once more, letting go of clasped hands, and floating arms downward to either side, returning to starting position.

16. Turning to Look at the Moon

While sitting, put your left arm behind your back at waist level. Place your right hand on your left knee and twist your body to the left, looking above and behind you. Repeat this on the opposite side for one repetition. Do each side three times and return to starting position.

Moving Practice

17. Gather and Play the Harp

While standing, bend your knees slowly while gathering your energy in a round sweeping motion with both arms. As you bring your arms upward, lift your right knee and slowly place your heel to the ground in front of you. Your arms extend in front of your body with your left hand at right elbow level. Arms and feet move in unison. Step back to starting position, gather energy again and repeat on the opposite side, landing softly on your left heel while extending your arms, right hand at elbow level, for a total of three repetitions on each side.

18. Gathering Your Energy

From standing position, gather your energy toward the top of your head and draw down the front side of your body. Gather again and hold your hands in front of your eyes. Lower your arms down to the chest position and hold. Next, lower your arms down to the lower Dan Tien, below the belly button, position and hold. Finally, relax hands to original start position.

Daily practice of qi gong is key to a healthy back, and possessing a strong back is the foundation to an active and fulfilling life. For further assistance, refer to the instructional DVD: Qi Gong for a Healthy Back, available at wellnesslivingstore.com

Advanced Practice

Lying Down practice
(Upon waking and before bedtime)

1. Awaken From Sleep
As your neck comes up to gaze at your toes, which are now flexed toward your head, reach down with your hands to the side of your legs. Hold this position for a few seconds and repeat three times.

2. Stretch Ankles and Straighten Legs
Bring your left knee to your chest and grasp with both hands. Rotate your ankle three times one way and three times the other way. Straighten your leg with the sole of your foot toward the ceiling and slowly return your leg back to starting position. Repeat three times on both sides.

3. Stretching Knees Like A Butterfly Opening Wings
Bring your knee to your chest, and grasp with both hands. While doing this movement bring your chin to your knee. Straighten your leg with the sole of your foot toward the ceiling and slowly return to starting position. Repeat three times on both sides.

Part two: Bring both legs to your chest and grasp with both hands. Bring your chin to your chest and release. Raise the soles of your feet to the ceiling and lower your legs back to starting position. Repeat three times.

4. Raise Legs and Ride a Bicycle
From a lying position, raise both legs toward your chest. Pedal like you would riding a bicycle, extending your alternating legs toward the floor and back again.

5. Lift the Mountain

From a lying position, bend your knees and place your feet closer to your hips. Your hands are on the floor, palm side down, next to your hips. Raise your body off the floor by pushing with your legs and extending your hips. Hold for a count of five and slowly lower yourself, feeling each vertebra release to the floor. Repeat for three repetitions.

6. Wriggle like a Young Dragon

From a sitting position, extend one leg with the opposite leg planted on the floor close to you. Your hands will be on the floor behind you, palm side down. Push with your planted foot while extending your hip to the ceiling, creating a table-like position. Head stays in a neutral position, with your eyes looking toward the ceiling at the apex of the move. Repeat three times on each side.

7. Stretch like a Cat

Kneel on your legs with your feet tucked under your hips and buttocks. Bring your chin to the floor with your arms outstretched in front of you. Transition forward to a cat stance with your hands underneath your shoulders and stretch your back to the sky, while tucking your pelvis underneath and your chin into your chest. Transition back to starting position and repeat for a total of three times.

8. Massage Kidneys in Circles

Sitting on your knees with your feet under your hips, massage your kidney area at the lower lumbar area. Repeat for about 50 circles.

9. Swim Like a Fish

Lay face down with your forehead on the floor and your hands by your sides. Lift your left leg as high as it will go, hold for two seconds, lower and repeat on the opposite side. Do three repetitions on each side.

10. Squat Like a Frog

Squat with feet wider than hips distance apart, feet point outward at 45 degrees. Place elbows inside your knees with hands touching the ground if possible. Straighten your back, with eyes gazing forward. Hold for 1-2 minutes.

Standing Practice

11. Weeping Willow Sways in the Morning Breeze

Stand feet hips-width apart, pelvis tucked slightly under, chin back with your eyes pointing forward. Bring your feet together. Cup hands in front of your navel area. Slowly rotate your head and neck three times one way and repeat in the opposite direction.

12. Great Elephant Lifts its Trunk

Begin with your feet close together. Round your back as you reach forward, palms down, in a circular motion to gather energy. As you pull your arms in toward your body, palms now turned upward, arch your back and rock onto your toes, pushing your belt line forward. Your arms continue to pull the energy behind you as you prepare to round your back and reach forward again, repeating this movement nine times.

As you finish the ninth movement, begin lowering into a squat position while gathering energy with both arms moving in circles toward one another. Lower your head and begin to rise slowly, one vertebrae at a time. Make an eagle's beak with each hand, all four fingers touching your thumbs, and slowly pull them vertically up the front of your body to throat level, fingers pointing down. Lower to your belt line, then rise vertically again to above your head while rising to your toes. Do this three times, lower your arms, and return to starting position.

13. Water and Fire Meet

Bend at the waist as you bring your hands to meet the inside of your shins. In a circular motion, massage the insides of your shin from your inner ankle to your inner upper thigh. Slowly rise, with hands pointing down vertically, to your heart center. Make circles with your elbows, upwards and back, while rising to your toes each time, then repeat, going in the opposite direction. Now make circles with one elbow at a time, twisting from the waist to accentuate the movement. Repeat three times on each side. Bring your elbows upward and back, back to center, upwards and back again. this time your hands will be further away from your shoulders. Return to center and repeat with your your arms fully extended to the sides with fingers pointed up. Allow your arms to relax and drop them back to your sides to finish.

14. Pushing the Mountain

Begin with your feet close together. Use both arms to make three wide circles, starting from your hip, to your shoulders, over your head, and complete the circle in a sweeping motion. At the end of the third repetition, take a large step out to the side and while transferring weight to the extended leg, push your arms like you are holding a giant boulder overhead, stretching the sides of your body over the extended leg. Shift your weight back and repeat pushing the mountain three times. At the end of the last push, begin three circles in the opposite position while returning to the original starting stance. Step out to the side again and push the mountain to the opposite side three more times. Return to starting position.

15. Jade Plate Receives Morning Dew

With heels together and toes pointed 45 degrees outward, touch your right thumb and forefingers together and place at your lower lumbar spine with fingers pointing upwards. With your left hand, move your arm across your belt line, palm side up, and make a circle going away from your body toward your left side, with hand finishing palm up by the left ear. Push your palm to the sky while pushing down with your right hand toward the floor. Do this movement three times and repeat on the opposite side.

16. Beauty Admires Herself in the Pond

With your feet shoulder-width apart, make clockwise circles with your arms from your waist to over your head three times. Toward the top of the third repetition, your right hand stays under your left arm, with your hand flexed away from you. Your left extends behind your head, with your elbow pointing skyward, and your hand flexed away from your midline. Look toward your right foot and push both arms on opposite directions. Do this three times. Repeat on the opposite side beginning with circles in a counterclockwise direction. Place your right hand behind your head, your left hand under your arms and press in opposite directions three times.

17. Crane Stretches its Body to Look Up

With your feet wider than shoulder width, bend from the waist, place your right hand on your knee and grab behind the right ankle with your left hand. Bend your legs and straighten your right knee, putting your weight on your bent left knee, while twisting from the waist and looking upward. Repeat on each side for a total of three times.

18. Guarding Plum Flower

Stand on one leg while hugging the opposite knee to your chest. Pull upward on your knee, toward your chest, three times and switch legs. Repeat on the opposite side.

19. Flying Crane Gracefully Lands

With feet slightly wider than shoulder-width apart, begin squatting while placing your palms on your lumbar/kidney area. While rising, with a faster motion, sweep your hands upward to end in front of your body at eye level, palm side down. Squat while slowly lowering your hands to the top of your knees. Repeat the kidney-sweeping motion upward while rising, and return to the squat position with hands on knees. Repeat once more for a total of three times.

Chair Sitting Practice

20. Solid as a Mountain
Sit toward the front of the chair, with knees bent around 90 degrees, pelvis tucked under and chin inwards with head erect. Sit for one minute, breathing through your abdomen.

21. Huddle Your Thighs
Bend forward to touch hands to the floor, head hanging between your knees. Breathe slowly through your abdomen. Return to starting position.

22. Stretch Body to Look Up
Reach with your right hand across to your left outer ankle, with your left hand resting your left knee. Twist from the waist while applying gentle pressure with your hands to assist the twist. Look up and behind you at the top of the movement. Repeat each side three times.

23. Arms Stretch Behind
Clasp your wrist behind your back and lean forward from the waist, gently pulling your arms upward to the sky. Your head hangs between your knees in this position for a count of five. Repeat this movement three times.

24. Arms Stretch Above and to the Sides
While sitting, clasp your hands in front of your chest and extend them overhead. Next, draw your hands down to chin level, and extend your arms upward to the left, and then again to the right. Finish by extending your arms overhead once more, letting go of clasped hands, and floating arms downward to either side, returning to starting position.

25. Turning to Look at the Moon
While sitting, put your left arm behind your back at waist level. Place your right hand on your left knee and twist your body to the left, looking above and behind you. Repeat this on the opposite side for one repetition. Do each side three times and return to starting position.

Moving Practice

26. Gather and Play the Harp

While standing, bend your knees slowly while gathering your energy in a round sweeping motion with both arms. As you bring your arms upward, lift your right knee and slowly place your heel to the ground in front of you. Your arms extend in front of your body with your left hand at right elbow level. Arms and feet move in unison. Step back to starting position, gather your energy again and repeat on the opposite side, landing softly on your left heel while extending your arms, right hand at elbow level, for a total of three repetitions on each side.

27. Cloud Hands

With feet shoulder-width apart, raise your left hand to eye level, palm facing your chest. The right hand circles behind you from your waist to your ear and moves forward to glide over the top of the opposite outstretched palm. Turn your right hand palm side up and twist from the waist and repeat on the opposite side. Do each side three times.

28. Gathering Your Energy

From standing position, gather your energy toward the top of your head and draw down the front side of your body. Gather again and hold your hands in front of your eyes.

Lower your arms down to the chest position and hold. Next, lower your arms down to the lower Dan Tien, below the belly button, position and hold. Finally, relax hands to original start position. Daily practice of qi gong is key to a healthy back, and possessing a strong back is the foundation to an active and fulfilling life. For further assistance, refer to the instructional DVD: Qi Gong for a Healthy Back, available at wellnesslivingstore.com.

Chapter Seven

Assume the Right Position: Optimum Biomechanics at Work, Home and Play

Applying proper body mechanics is essential to injury and pain prevention. It is the understanding and coordination of movement and weight distribution throughout the body. Correct alignment or posture is a key component to proper body mechanics. Since posture affects all aspects of the back's muscles, tendons, ligaments and skeletal frame, consistently incorrect posture will most likely lead to back injury. The good news is that correcting posture can help heal and prevent back injury. This empowers us to take an active role in the recovery from back injury and in the prevention of recurring back pain.

The tricky thing about body mechanics is that bad postural habits can very often be so ingrained in our daily lives that these habits actually feel right. Be aware that just because a postural habit feels comfortable does not necessarily mean it is correct. On the contrary, such habits can be very damaging, for they can put excessive strain and stress on the back, leaving it vulnerable to injury.

Good Posture Starts With the Neck

A fundamental approach to addressing chronic neck pain is correcting your posture. Try positioning your head directly above your neck, your ear lobes aligned with your shoulders and the apex of your skull effortlessly piercing the sky as if being lifted by a floating balloon. This position is ideal because it requires the least amount of neck exertion in the upright position. Of course, you will not maintain the position at all times. The key is to return to this posture whenever possible to prevent overworking the neck. By regulating stress on the neck, we can slow down the degeneration of the neck joints.

Taking a few minutes to gently move and stretch the neck and trapezius after every two hours of work is another habit that can be effective in resolving and preventing neck tension. Refer to the warm up exercises for the neck described in chapter five.

The Four Curvatures of the Spine

To understand alignment of the back, we must review the four natural curves of the spine mentioned earlier: cervical lordosis, thoracic kyphosis, lumbar lordosis and sacral kyphosis. Lordosis is inward curvature and kyphosis is outward curvature. A small degree of curvature in these four primary areas of the spine is essential for correct weight distribution. Without these natural curves, too much strain would be put on your muscles, tendons and ligaments. Too much curving, on the other hand, puts an overload of pressure on the joints of the back. The four curves should be just enough to maintain a balanced alignment of the back.

You should constantly strive for optimum alignment of the back while sitting, standing and moving through life. Good posture will distribute weight evenly and minimize harmful levels of pressure in localized areas of the back. Practicing good body mechanics is fundamentally beneficial for both the recovery from back pain and for the prevention of recurring pain.

When alignment is optimum, muscles, tendons and ligaments are not overstretched nor overly tensed to the point of exhaustion, fatigue and injury. Optimum alignment also ensures that the pressure on the various joints of the back is even, for when joints receive excessive pressure, they are more prone to injury.

Use Your Body Correctly to Prevent Injury

Many patients inadvertently injure themselves in their day-to-day activities. For instance, twisting while carrying a load is a common cause of back injury. You may do this while carrying a baby out of a car seat or while transferring laundry from the washer to the dryer. When transferring weight, it is safer to face it straight on with no twist in the torso before attempting to lift and move it. Making quick, sudden movements is another common cause of back pain. Such movements are required while participating in sporting events, but if the body is not conditioned to make such quick movements, injury can result. Also, making sudden movements can occur in daily life outside of sports, such as when trying to catch a falling object. Be aware that doing such a sudden movement when the body is not conditioned for it can lead to injury.

Stand Like a Tree

Correct standing posture begins with positioning the crown of your head to be perpendicular with the sky. Stand as if there is a string pulling you up from the crown. Make the chin parallel to the floor and position the shoulders directly below the ear lobes so that both sides are level. Both sides of your hips should be level, with your weight distributed to both sides evenly. Position the kneecaps so that they face forward and are slightly bent and not locked. Let your hands hang to the sides slightly in front of the thighs. Visualize your feet rooting into the ground and stand like a tree.

Sit Like a Mountain

Correct sitting posture begins with positioning the pelvis in a neutral position, tilting neither backward nor forward. Focus your weight on the sit bones or ischium of the pelvis and not on the sacrum or lower back. Maintain a straight and stable back and resist slouching. Position your legs so that they have a 90-degee bend, with the feet firmly planted on the ground. Folding your legs is fine as long it provides stability and promotes erect and relaxed back muscles. Never cross your legs as it throws off your alignment and hampers circulation. Visualize being a mountain with the highest peak as your head and the lower ridges as your shoulders, sitting solidly and confidently.

Sit Properly While Working at Your Desk

When working at your desk, position your feet flat on the floor or on a foot-rest. Consider using a lower back support if working for an extended period of time. Maintain a 90-degree angle or greater between the thighs and the back and a 90-degree angle flexion of the legs. It's important to also have a 90-degree angle flexion of your arms if working on a computer keyboard. Align hands, wrists and forearms along a straight line. Position your computer monitor slightly below eye level and avoid crossing your legs. Working with your hands as the legs are crossed causes the pelvis to tilt excessively forward, which compresses the curve of the lower back and causes excessive pressure on those joints and possible injury. Never bend your neck laterally to hold the phone between your ear and shoulder. Finally, remain hydrated to keep muscles from becoming too tense.

Standing Up is an Out-standing Option

We recommend adjustable-height desks to our patients suffering from neck and lower back pain. Try adjusting your desk up when you work on the computer, maintaining the same posture with your upper body as if sitting: a 90-degree angle flexion of your arms if working on a computer keyboard, aligning your hands, wrists and forearms along a straight line. Position your computer monitor slightly below eye level so that your neck is not unduly strained. Position your head as if there is a string pulling you up from the crown. Pull your chin inward and position the shoulders directly below the ear lobes so that both sides are level. Both sides of your hips should be level, with your weight distributed to both sides evenly. Position your kneecaps so that they face forward and are slightly bent and not locked. If you get tired you may alternate your weight from one side to the other, but always return to being evenly planted with both feet on the ground.

Don't Let Your Back Be Aggravated by Driving

With long hours of commuting in stressful traffic situations, it is no wonder many people feel worse with their back pain after driving. Move the seat so that the foot can reach all the pedals without having to fully extend the legs in a locked position. Adjust the headrest to a position that is aligned to the head for neck protection. Wear your seat belt and position the buttocks to the back of the seat to ensure optimum support and good posture. If you are in a comfortable and ergonomically correct position, you can eliminate the aches and pains you experience now.

Don't Let Flying Throw off Your Back

Long hours sitting in a cramped seat on an airplane is guaranteed to worsen your back. However, if you follow the advice here you can lessen or eliminate pain. First, when seated position your buttocks to the back of the seat to ensure optimum support and good posture. Place a small cushion or rolled-up blanket between the lower back and the back of the seat. Do the pelvic tilt from the seated position by pressing the small of your back against the back of the chair, allowing the pelvis to tilt up while exhaling. Upon inhalation, relax the back. Do the chest expansion from the seated position by expanding the chest and bringing the shoulder blades together while inhaling and upon exhalation, relax. Repeat the above two or three times.

Get up periodically and stand or walk up and down the aisle.

If You Have to Push, Use Your Body

Whenever possible, push rather than pull a heavy object if you need to move it. When pushing an object, maintain a slight bend in the knees. Keep the neck and back properly aligned before and during the exertion of force. Instead of only using your hands and arm muscles, engage your whole body, including your trunk and legs. Whenever possible get someone to help you instead of moving heavy objects by yourself to avoid injury.

If You Have to Lift, Bend Your Knees

Whenever possible break up a heavy load to several lighter ones to minimize risk of injury.

Never try to lift a load that is too heavy for you to lift alone. Whenever possible, ask for help. When lifting, use a trolley for transporting heavy loads. Before lifting the object, face it straight on. Maintain a straight and stable back. Bend from the knees in a squat position with one foot slightly in front of the other and the object positioned between the knees. Grasp the object from underneath with both hands, arms straightened, with the object positioned close or against the torso. Lean slightly forward from the hips, maintain a straight spine and take most of the weight in the legs. Extend from the legs, keeping the load in your arms pressed close to the torso. Never lift while in a twisted position and avoid rounding the back. Be cautious when setting an object down and repeat the steps above in reverse.

Conclusion

For over 30 years we have been busy treating thousands of patients with back pain. It is by far the most common problem we see in our clinics. We have offered each of our patients the treatment modalities mentioned in the book—acupuncture, tuina bodywork, herbal and nutritional therapies, and ergonomic consultations. We have also coached our patients in mind-body balance with meditation and qi gong. Most of our patients have gotten better with their back pain through these time-tested therapeutic procedures and restored their full and active lifestyles. Many have avoided unnecessary surgery.

It is our hope that we have produced a user-friendly book on the care and maintenance of the back so that people everywhere, and not just our patients can benefit from this 5,000 year-old medical and wellness tradition. If you are in Southern California we invite you make an appointment in the office nearest you for treatment of your back problem and join us for Qi Gong for Back Health classes in our offices. If you are trying out the exercises outlined in this book we recommend that you practice them with the instructional DVD (order at wellnesslivingstore.com) and let us know how they've helped you. Email us at contact@taoofwellness.com

Thank you.

Dr. Mao Shing Ni & Albert Vaca
Tao of Wellness

Index

A

Appendix I

Case Study I

For 18 months leading up to our initial meeting, a 39-year-old female had been suffering from periodic episodes of acute back pain and spasm that radiated to the right buttock and right hamstring muscles. In conjunction to periodic back pain and spasm, she also experienced a pulling sensation in her right calf muscle and at the topside (dorsum) of her right foot, especially at her second, third, and fourth toes.

She had received an x-ray of her lower back that was inconclusive. Her primary care physician had recently diagnosed her with sciatica and prescribed her NSAIDS and a muscle relaxant. Although she did receive temporary relief, the periodic pain episodes persisted.

This patient was working as a teacher and stood for most of the day. She had also been a dancer and an avid runner in the past. Also noted was her tendency not to drink enough water.

After the initial evaluation, we proceeded with a series of six acupuncture visits at one visit per week, combined with six weeks of herbal therapy, anti-inflammatory foods and improved hydration throughout the day.

By the second treatment, her pain had decreased noticeably, and by the fourth treatment, the pain had decreased by up to 85%. By the fifth week, she had no pain. The last two treatments of the series of six were designed to prevent the pain from returning. By the end of the sixth and final treatment of the series, she continued to be pain-free.

Case Study II

For six months leading up to our initial meeting, a 71-year-old female had been experiencing left-side lower back pain that had progressed to radiating pain down the left buttock and leg. Upon examination we confirmed it to be sciatica.

The pain intensified leading up to the first visit, progressing from a chronic stiffness to a sharp, burning pain that began at the left side of the third lumbar vertebra, the sacrum and the left leg. The x-ray showed severe facet degeneration from the third lumbar vertebra to the sacrum. The x-ray also showed retrolisthesis. Retrolisthesis is the opposite of spondylolisthesis. Unlike spondylolisthesis in which a vertebra slips forward, retrolisthesis is when a vertebra slips back. The consequent nerve root compression from facet degeneration and retrolisthesis manifested as severe sciatica.

Estrogen has been found to have protective effects on cartilage by virtue of its anti-inflammatory properties, according to a study published in the April 2008 journal "Clinical and Experimental Immunology." This patient had been menopausal for about 20 years. This implies that she may have had less estrogen and therefore more joint degeneration and inflammation. The treatment principle was to promote circulation, reduce inflammation and support and restore healthy hormonal function in the body.

Our treatment plan for the patient consisted of acupuncture, tuina bodywork, Chinese herbal therapy and qi gong exercise. Her treatment course lasted three months at once a week intervals for acupuncture and tuina bodywork. An herbal formula was customized for her to support her body's own regenerative abilities to produce estrogen. Her pain reduced about 20 percent immediately after the first treatment. After the fourth treatment, the radiating pain down the leg had subsided completely, and only a tolerable lower back soreness remained. After the seventh treatment, her lower back pain decreased and became more localized to the left sacroiliac joint. After the tenth treatment, the patient was virtually pain-free.

Appendix II

Acupuncture for Back Pain Studies (10)

Aranha, M. F. M., Alves, M. C., Bérzin, F., & Gavião, M. B. D. (October 01, 2011). Efficacy of electroacupuncture for myofascial pain in the upper trapezius muscle: a case series. Revista Brasileira De Fisioterapia, 15, 5, 371-379.

Abstract

Background: Electroacupunture (EA) includes the passage of an electrical current through the acupuncture needle and is commonly used for pain relief.

Objective: To evaluate the EA treatment effects for myofascial pain in the upper trapezius muscle.

Methods: Twenty women aged ranging from 18 to 40 years (mean=24.95; SD=5.88 years), with a body mass index ranging from 19 to 25 kg/m2 (mean=22.33; SD=0.56 kg/m2), with regular menstrual cycles controlled by oral contraceptive, local or referred pain for more than six months and at least one myofascial trigger point in the upper trapezius participated in this study. The participants received a total of nine EA sessions over five weeks. The needles were inserted at the acupoints GB20, GB21, LV3, LI4, and at "ashi" points. A mixed current of 2 Hz and 100 Hz was applied alternatively every 5 seconds for 30 minutes. The outcomes were pain intensity measured by the visual analogue scale (VAS), pressure pain threshold (PPT) measured by an algometer, electromyography (EMG) and quality of life measured by the SF-36 questionnaire. Inter-occurrences between sessions were monitored. Paired t-test, Wilcoxon test, and repeated measure analysis of variance (ANOVA) having Tukey-Kramer as post-hoc tests were used.

Results: Significant improvement in pain intensity and in PPT occurred after treatment (P<0.0001). EMG of the right trapezius during contraction increased significantly, suggesting muscle function enhancement; the quality of life improved, related to physical components of the SF-36 (P<0.05).

Conclusion: The EA showed to be a reliable method for myofascial pain relief. Large randomized blinded controlled trials might be carried out to confirm these results. Article registered in the Registro Brasileiro de Ensaios Clínicos under number RBR-4hb6f6.

Carlsson, C. P., & Sjölund, B. H. (January 01, 2001). Acupuncture for chronic low back pain: a randomized placebo-controlled study with long-term follow-up. The Clinical Journal of Pain, 17, 4, 296-305.

Abstract

Objective: The authors sought to determine whether a series of needle acupuncture treatments produced long-term relief of chronic low back pain.

Design: A blinded placebo-controlled study with an independent observer. The patients were randomized to receive manual acupuncture, electroacupuncture, or active placebo (mock transcutaneous electrical nerve stimulation). Subjects were examined and monitored by an investigator who was blinded to the treatment given.

Setting: A tertiary-level pain clinic at a Swedish university hospital.

Patients: Fifty consecutive patients (33 women, 17 men; mean age, 49.8 years) with chronic low back pain (mean pain duration, 9.5 years) and without rhizopathy or history of acupuncture treatment were included in the study.

Interventions: Treatments were given once per week for 8 weeks. Two further treatments were given during the follow-up assessment period of 6 months or longer.

Outcome Measures: The independent observer made a global assessment of the patients 1, 3, and 6 months after treatment. The patients kept pain diaries to score pain intensity twice daily, analgesic intake, and quality of sleep daily, and activity level weekly.

Results: At the 1-month independent assessment, 16 of 34 patients in the acupuncture groups and 2 of 16 patients in the placebo group showed improvement (p <0.05). At the 6-month follow-up assessment, 14 of 34 patients in the acupuncture groups and 2 of 16 patients in the placebo group showed improvement (p <0.05). A significant decrease in pain intensities occurred at 1 and 3 months in the acupuncture groups compared with the placebo group. There was a significant improvement in return to work, quality of sleep, and analgesic intake in subjects treated with acupuncture.

Conclusions: The authors found a long-term pain-relieving effect of needle acupuncture compared with true placebo in some patients with chronic nociceptive low back pain.

Ekdahl, L., & Petersson, K. (March 01, 2010). Acupuncture treatment of pregnant women with low back and pelvic pain - an intervention study. Scandinavian Journal of Caring Sciences, 24, 1, 175-182.

Abstract
Objective: To describe patients' experience of acupuncture treatment in low back and pelvic pain during pregnancy.

Design: An intervention study carried out between September 2000 and December 2001, involving 40 pregnant women.

Participants: The   study   population   consisted   of healthy pregnant women presenting with low back and pelvic pain at maternity health care centres within a defined area in southern Sweden.

Intervention: Two groups of women received acupuncture treatment from gestational week 20 (group 1) or week 26 (group 2) respectively, for a period of 6 weeks divided into eight sessions of 30 minutes each.

Measurements: Pain assessment was carried out using Pain-O-Meter and visual analogue scale (POM-VAS), Short-Form McGill Questionnaire (SF-MPQ), Short-Form-36: Health Survey Questionnaire (SF-36), followed by telephone interviews 2-3 months after delivery.

Findings: The results of POM-VAS, SF-MPQ and SF-36 showed a relief of pain in both groups. In group 2, an improvement in several SF-36 variables was noted in spite of increased physical restrictions. Telephone interviews confirmed that expectations of treatment were fulfilled. Using content analysis the main category, limitations in daily life, was identified, with subcategories pain, and psychological well-being.

Conclusion: It may be advantageous to begin acupuncture therapy later in pregnancy to maximize pain relief.

Grant, D. J., Bishop-Miller, J., Winchester, D. M., Anderson, M., & Faulkner, S. (January 01, 1999). A randomized comparative trial of acupuncture versus transcutaneous electrical nerve stimulation for chronic back pain in the elderly. Pain, 82, 1, 9-13.

Abstract

Sixty patients aged 60 or over with back pain for at least 6 months were recruited from General Practitioner referrals and randomized to 4 weeks of treatment with acupuncture or transcutaneous electrical nerve stimulation (TENS). All treatments were administered by the same physiotherapist and both groups had the same contact with him. The following were measured at baseline, completion and at a 3-month follow-up by an independent observer blinded to treatment received: (1) pain severity on visual analogue scale (VAS); (2) pain subscale of Nottingham Health Profile (NHP); (3) number of analgesic tablets consumed in previous week; (4) spinal flexion from C7 to S1. Thirty-two patients were randomized to acupuncture and 28 to TENS; only three withdrew (two from acupuncture, one from TENS). Significant improvements were shown on VAS ($P < 0.001$), NHP ($P < 0.001$) and tablet count ($P < 0.05$) between baseline and completion in both groups, these improvements remaining significant comparing baseline with follow-up with a further non-significant improvement in VAS and NHP in the acupuncture group. The acupuncture but not the TENS patients showed a small but statistically significant improvement ($P < 0.05$) in mean spinal flexion between baseline and completion which was not maintained at follow-up. Thus in these elderly patients with chronic back pain both acupuncture and TENS had demonstratable benefits which outlasted the treatment period. Acupuncture may improve spinal flexion. This trial cannot exclude the possibility that both treatments are 'placebos.'

Itoh, K., Itoh, S., Katsumi, Y., & Kitakoji, H. (February 01, 2009). A pilot study on using acupuncture and transcutaneous electrical nerve stimulation to treat chronic non-specific low back pain. Complementary Therapies in Clinical Practice, 15, 1, 22-25.

Abstract

Objective: The present study tests whether a combined treatment of acupuncture and transcutaneous electrical nerve stimulation (TENS) is more effective than acupuncture or TENS alone for treating chronic low back pain (LBP).

Methods: Thirty-two patients with chronic LBP were randomly allocated to four groups. The acupuncture group (ACP) received only acupuncture treatment at selected acupoints for low back pain; the TENS group (TENS) received only TENS treatment at pain areas; the acupuncture and TENS group (A&T) received both acupuncture and TENS treatments; the control group (CT) received topical poultice (only when necessary). Each group received specific weekly treatment five times during the study. Outcome measures were pain intensity in terms of visual analogue scale (VAS) and QOL of low back in terms of Roland-Morris Disability Questionnaire (RDQ).

Results: The ACP, TENS and A&T groups all reported lower VAS and RDQ scores. Significant reduction in pain intensity (P<0.008) and significant improvement in QOL (P<0.008) were shown in the A&T group.

Conclusion: Combined acupuncture and TENS treatment is effective in pain relief and QOL of low back improvement for the sampled patients suffering from chronic LBP.

Macdonald, A. J., Macrae, K. D., Master, B. R., & Rubin, A. P. (January 01, 1983). Superficial acupuncture in the relief of chronic low back pain. Annals of the Royal College of Surgeons of England, 65, 1, 44-6.

Abstract

A single-blind, randomized, placebo-controlled trial of superficial acupuncture in the treatment of low back pain was carried out by comparing 8 patients treated by acupuncture with 9 patients treated by placebo. In all five measures of efficacy chosen for study the acupuncture group achieved better responses than the placebo group; four of the five inter-group differences were statistically significant. In addition, an overall mean for all five measures combined showed significant superiority of acupuncture over placebo.

Meng, C. F., Wang, D., Ngeow, J., Lao, L., Peterson, M., & Paget, S. (December 01, 2003). Acupuncture for chronic low back pain in older patients: a randomized, controlled trial. Rheumatology, 42, 12, 1508-1517.

Abstract

Objective: To determine if acupuncture is an effective, safe adjunctive treatment to standard therapy for chronic low back pain (LBP) in older patients.

Methods: The inclusion criteria for subjects were: (i) LBP > or = 12 weeks and (ii) age > or = 60 yr; the exclusion criteria were (i) spinal tumour, infection or fracture and (ii) associated neurological symptoms. The subjects were randomized to two groups. The control group of subjects continued their usual care as directed by their physicians, i.e. NSAIDs, muscle relaxants, paracetamol and back exercises. Subjects in the acupuncture group in addition received biweekly acupuncture with electrical stimulation for 5 weeks. Outcome was measured by the modified Roland Disability Questionnaire (RDQ) at weeks 0, 2, 6 and 9. The primary outcome measure was changed in RDQ score between weeks 0 and 6.

Results: Fifty-five patients were enrolled, with eight drop-outs. Twenty-four subjects were randomized to the acupuncture group and 23 were randomized to the control group. Acupuncture subjects had a significant decrease in RDQ score of 4.1 +/- 3.9 at week 6, compared with a mean decrease of 0.7 +/- 2.8 in the control group (P = 0.001). This effect was maintained for up to 4 weeks after treatment at week 9, with a decrease in RDQ of 3.5 +/- 4.4 from baseline, compared with 0.43 +/- 2.7 in the control group (P = 0.007). The mean global transition score was higher in the acupuncture group, 3.7 +/- 1.2, indicating greater improvement, compared with the score in the control group, 2.5 +/- 0.9 (P < 0.001). Fewer acupuncture subjects had medication-related side-effects compared with the control group.

Conclusions: Acupuncture is an effective, safe adjunctive treatment for chronic LBP in older patients.

Molsberger, A. F., Mau, J., Pawelec, D. B., & Winkler, J. (January 01, 2002). Does acupuncture improve the orthopedic management of chronic low back pain--a randomized, blinded, controlled trial with 3 months follow up. Pain, 99, 3, 579-87.

Abstract

This prospective, randomized controlled trial, with three parallel groups, patient and observer blinded for verum and sham acupuncture and a follow-up of 3 months raises the question: "Does a combination of acupuncture and conservative orthopedic treatment improve conservative orthopedic treatment in chronic low back pain (LBP)?" 186 in-patients of a LBP rehabilitation center with a history of LBP > or = 6 weeks, VAS > or = 50mm, and no pending compensation claims, were selected; for the three random groups 4 weeks of treatment was applied. 174 patients met the protocol criteria and reported after treatment, 124 reported after 3 months follow-up. Patients were assorted 4 strata: chronic LBP, < or = 0.5 years, 0.5-2 years, 2-5 years, > or = 5 years. Analysis was by intention to treat. Group 1 (Verum+COT) received 12 treatments of verum acupuncture and conservative orthopedic treatment (COT). Group 2 (Sham+COT) received 12 treatments of non-specific needling and COT. Group 3 (nil+COT) received COT alone. Verum and sham acupuncture were blinded against patient and examiner. The primary endpoints were pain reduction > or = 50% on VAS 3 months after the end of the treatment protocol. Secondary endpoints were pain reduction > or = 50% on VAS and treatment efficacy on a four-point box scale directly after the end of the treatment protocol and treatment efficacy after 3 months. In the whole sample a pain relief of > or = 50% on VAS was reported directly after the end of treatment protocol: Verum+COT 65% (95%CI 51-77%), Sham+COT 34% (95%CI 22-49%), nil+COT 43% (95%CI29-58%) results are significant for Verum+COT over Sham+COT (P<or= 0.02). The results after 3 months are: Verum+COT 77% (95%CI 62-88%), Sham+COT 29% (95%CI 16-46%), nil+COT 14% (95%CI 4-30%)—effects are significant for Verum+COT over Sham+COT (P<or= 0.001) and for Verum+COT over nil+COT (P<0.001). No difference was found in the mobility of the patients nor in the intake of NSAID diclofenac. Our conclusion is that acupuncture can be an important supplement of conservative orthopedic treatment in the management of chronic LBP.

Weidenhammer, W., Linde, K., Streng, A., Hoppe, A., & Melchart, D. (January 01, 2007). Acupuncture for chronic low back pain in routine care: a multicenter observational study. The Clinical Journal of Pain, 23, 2, 128-35.

Abstract

Objective: To investigate patient characteristics and outcomes after undergoing acupuncture treatment for chronic low back pain (CLBP) in Germany and to analyze chronification, pain grading, and depression as predictors for treatment outcomes.

Patients and Methods: Patients with CLBP (ICD-10 diagnoses M54.4 or M54.5) who underwent acupuncture therapy (mean number of sessions 8.7+/-2.9) within the framework of a reimbursement and research program sponsored by German statutory sickness funds were included in an observational study. Patients were asked to complete detailed questionnaires that included questions on intensity and frequency of pain and instruments measuring functional ability, depression, and quality of life (SF-36) before and after treatment and 6 months after beginning acupuncture. Participating physicians assessed pain chronification in patients.

Results: A total of 2564 patients (mean age 57.7+/-14.0 y, 78.7% female), who were treated by 1607 physicians, were included in the main analysis. After 6 months (6-mo follow-up), 45.5% of patients demonstrated clinically significant improvements in their functional ability scores. The mean number of days with pain was decreased by half (from 21 to 10 d/ mo). Employed patients (employed patient subgroup analysis) reported a 30% decrease from baseline in days of work lost. In all, 8.1% of patients reported adverse events, the majority of which were minor. Subgroup analyses focusing on pain severity, stage of chronification, and depression revealed statistically significant relationships both to baseline measures and to reduction of pain after acupuncture.

Conclusions: Acupuncture treatment is associated with clinically relevant improvements in patients suffering from CLBP of varying degrees of chronification and/or severity.

Witt, C. M., Jena, S., Selim, D., Brinkhaus, B., Reinhold, T., Wruck, K., Liecker, B., Linde, K., Wegscheider, K., & Willich, S. N. (January 01, 2006). Pragmatic Randomized Trial Evaluating the Clinical and Economic Effectiveness of Acupuncture for Chronic Low Back Pain. American Journal of Epidemiology, 164, 5, 487-496.

Abstract

In a randomized controlled trial plus a nonrandomized cohort, the authors investigated the effectiveness and costs of acupuncture in addition to routine care in the treatment of chronic low back pain and assessed whether the effects of acupuncture differed in randomized and nonrandomized patients. In 2001, German patients with chronic low back pain were allocated to an acupuncture group or a no-acupuncture control

group. Persons who did not consent to randomization were included in a nonrandomized acupuncture group. All patients were allowed to receive routine medical care in addition to study treatment. Back function (Hannover Functional Ability Questionnaire), pain, and quality of life were assessed at baseline and after 3 and 6 months, and cost-effectiveness was analyzed. Of 11,630 patients (mean age = 52.9 years (standard deviation, 13.7); 59% female), 1,549 were randomized to the acupuncture group and 1,544 to the control group; 8,537 were included in the nonrandomized acupuncture group. At 3 months, back function improved by 12.1 (standard error (SE), 0.4) to 74.5 (SE, 0.4) points in the acupuncture group and by 2.7 (SE, 0.4) to 65.1 (SE, 0.4) points among controls (difference = 9.4 points (95% confidence interval 8.3, 10.5); $p<0.001$). Nonrandomized patients had more severe symptoms at baseline and showed improvements in back function similar to those seen in randomized patients. The incremental cost-effectiveness ratio was euro10,526 (euros) per quality-adjusted life year. Acupuncture plus routine care was associated with marked clinical improvements in these patients and was relatively cost-effective.
Acupuncture for Back Pain Reviews (3)

Manheimer, E., White, A., Berman, B., Forys, K., & Ernst, E. (January 01, 2005). Meta-analysis: acupuncture for low back pain. Annals of Internal Medicine, 142, 8, 651-63.

Abstract

Background: Low back pain limits activity and is the second most frequent reason for physician visits. Previous research shows widespread use of acupuncture for low back pain.

Purpose: To assess acupuncture's effectiveness for treating low back pain.

Data Sources: Randomized, controlled trials were identified through searches of MEDLINE, Cochrane Central, EMBASE, AMED, CINAHL, CISCOM, and GERA databases through August 2004. Additional data sources included previous reviews and personal contacts with colleagues. Study Selection: Randomized, controlled trials comparing needle acupuncture with sham acupuncture, other sham treatments, no additional treatment, or another active treatment for patients with low back pain.

Data Extraction: Data were dually extracted for the outcomes of pain, functional status, overall improvement, return to work, and analgesic consumption. In addition, study quality was assessed.

Data Synthesis: The 33 randomized, controlled trials that met inclusion criteria were subgrouped according to acute or chronic pain, style of acupuncture, and type of control group used. The principal [correction] measure of effect size was the standardized mean difference, since the trials assessed the same outcome but measured it in various ways. For the primary outcome of short-term relief of chronic pain, the meta-analyses showed that acupuncture is significantly more effective than sham treatment (standardized mean difference, 0.54 [95% CI, 0.35 to 0.73]; 7 trials) and no additional treatment (standardized mean difference, 0.69 [CI, 0.40 to 0.98]; 8 trials). For patients with acute low back pain, data are sparse and inconclusive. Data are also insufficient for drawing conclusions about acupuncture's short-term effectiveness compared with most other therapies.

Limitations: The quantity and quality of the included trials varied.

Conclusions: Acupuncture effectively relieves chronic low back pain. No evidence suggests that acupuncture is more effective than other active therapies.

Trigkilidas, D. (October 01, 2010). Acupuncture therapy for chronic lower back pain: A systematic review. Annals of the Royal College of Surgeons of England, 92, 7, 595-598.

Abstract

Introduction: Chronic low back pain is a common condition affecting a significant proportion of the population and has large economic implications on the society. Acupuncture has grown in popularity as an alternative therapy for chronic low back pain. Recent National Institute for Health and Clinical Excellence (NICE) guidelines on low back pain offer a course of acupuncture as a baseline treatment option according to patient preference. The aim of this systematic review was to evaluate if this treatment option is justified in view of recent evidence available on the efficacy of acupuncture.

Materials and Methods: Studies included were identified by a PubMed search for relevant, randomised, controlled trials on the 23 July 2009. A systematic review was performed.

Results: Fifteen randomised controlled trials were identified. Of these, four met the eligibility criteria and were critically appraised. These trials suggest acupuncture can be superior to usual care in treating chronic low back pain, especially, when patients have positive expectations about acupuncture.

Conclusions: NICE guidelines of a course of acupuncture, offered according to patient preference as a treatment option for chronic low back pain, are justified.

Yuan, J., Purepong, N., Kerr, D. P., McDonough, S., Park, J., & Bradbury, I. (November 01, 2008). Effectiveness of acupuncture for low back pain: A systematic review.Spine, 33, 23.)

Abstract

Study Design: A systematic review of randomized controlled trials (RCTs).

Objective: To explore the evidence for the effectiveness of acupuncture for nonspecific low back pain (LBP).

Summary of Background Data: Since the most recent systematic reviews on RCTs on acupuncture for LBP, 6 RCTs have been published, which may impact on the previous conclusions.

Methods: Searches were completed for RCTs on all types of acupuncture for patients with nonspecific LBP published in English. Methodologic quality was scored using the Van Tulder scale. Trials were deemed to be high quality if they scored more than 6/11 on the Van Tulder scale, carried out appropriate statistical analysis, with at least 40 patients per group, and did not exceed 20% and 30% dropouts at short/intermediate and long-term follow-up, respectively. High quality trials were given more weight when conducting the best evidence synthesis. Studies were grouped according to the control interventions, i.e., no treatment, sham intervention, conventional therapy, acupuncture in addition to conventional therapy. Treatment effect size and clinical significance were also determined. The adequacy of acupuncture treatment was judged by comparison of recommendations made in textbooks, surveys, and reviews.

Results: Twenty-three trials (n = 6359) were included and classified into 5 types of comparisons, 6 of which were of high quality. There is moderate evidence that acupuncture is more effective than no treatment, and strong evidence of no significant difference between acupuncture and sham acupuncture, for short-term pain relief. There is strong evidence that acupuncture can be a useful supplement to other forms of conventional therapy for nonspecific LBP, but the effectiveness of acupuncture compared with other forms of conventional therapies still requires further investigation.

Conclusion: Acupuncture versus no treatment, and as an adjunct to conventional care, should be advocated in the European Guidelines for the treatment of chronic LBP.

Resources

Tao of Wellness Health Centers
www.taoofwellness.com

Santa Monica, CA
310-917-2200

Pasadena, CA
626-397-1000

Newport Beach, CA
949-706-7770

Tao of Wellness is an integrative medical center combining the best of Western medical diagnostics with Eastern medical treatment. Its focus is on treating the whole person—body, mind and spirit while helping discover and eliminate the causes of illness. It is renowned for its fertility, women's health, pain management, anti-aging and integrative oncology specialties utilizing acupuncture, tuina bodywork, herbal and nutritional therapies, and qi gong and meditation coaching.

The Wellness Living Store
800-772-0222; 310-260-0013
www.wellnesslivingstore.com
order@taostar.com

Nourishing Chinese herbal products from the 38th-generation Ni Family Healing tradition. Books on Taoist teachings to nurture the spirit and to provide tools for positive living. Tai Chi and qi gong on DVD, and guided meditation on CD. The Wellness Living Store also carries products and everything to make your life healthier.

Infinichi
www.infinichi.com

Personalized health and wellbeing company providing wellness products such as herbal formulas, teas and skincare as well as meditation and mind/body practices and self-coaching programs that support your individual Five Element Personality Type. Go to website and take the Five Element Quiz to discover your Element.

Yo San University
Traditional Chinese Medicine & Clinic
Los Angeles, CA
877-967-2648; 310-577-3000
www.yosan.edu
admissions@yosan.edu

One of the finest and most academically rigorous Traditional Chinese Medicine schools in the United States, Yo San University offers a fully accredited Master's and Doctoral degree programs in acupuncture, herbology, tuina body work, and qi movement arts. In this program, students explore their spiritual growth as an integral part of learning the healing arts.

Chi Health Institute
Los Angeles, CA
www.chihealth.org
contact@collegeoftao.com

The Chi Health Institute (CHI) offers classes and certification in the Ni family qi movement arts including tai chi, qi gong, and Taoist meditation.

College of Tao
Los Angeles, CA
www.collegeoftao.org
contact@collegeoftao.com

Learn about classical Taoist teachings transmitted by the Ni family through books, mentoring, and retreats organized by the College of Tao. The COT assists people in achieving physical, mental, and spiritual health by nurturing self-respect and by offering methods of self-improvement based on the principles in the classic works of the I Ching and Lao Tzu's Tao Teh Ching.

Chinese Nutrition: Distance Learning and Certification Course
www.taostar.com

Apply the classic concepts and power of Traditional Chinese Medicine to the selection of daily foods. Basic understanding and practical application of nutrition theories including food energetics, survey of Zang-Fu syndromes (organ systems), and patient consultation. Up to 45 hours of CEU credit available for licensed acupuncturists.

Infinichi Energy Healing
Los Angeles
www.collegeoftao.org/infinichi-energy-healing.html
contact@collegeoftao.com

Professional training in qi healing leading to certification as an Energy Healing Practitioner. The program is designed to develop your energetic healing abilities utilizing the Ni family books and texts that relate to Traditional Chinese Medicine, qi gong, Chinese bodywork, and natural spirituality. It features a progressive, systematic program that nurtures understanding, facilitates skill development, and promotes self-growth.

Acupuncture.com
www.acupuncture.com

Acupuncture.com is the gateway to Chinese medicine, health, and wellness. As a consumer, you can learn all about acupuncture and its research and search for a licensed practitioner near you and as a professional, explore in-depth information on acupuncture and herbal medicine and access resources to support your practice.